THE ART OF MAKING
GELATO

MORE THAN 50 FLAVORS
TO MAKE AT HOME

Morano Gelato

THE ART OF MAKING
GELATO

MORE THAN 50 FLAVORS
TO MAKE AT HOME

MORGAN MORANO

Race Point
PUBLISHING

Brimming with creative inspiration, how-to projects, and useful information to enrich your everyday life, Quarto Knows is a favorite destination for those pursuing their interests and passions. Visit our site and dig deeper with our books into your area of interest: Quarto Creates, Quarto Cooks, Quarto Homes, Quarto Lives, Quarto Drives, Quarto Explores, Quarto Gifts, or Quarto Kids.

Editor: Susan Sulich and Susan Lauzau
Designer: Tim Palin Creative

Photography by Chad Finer except for the following: Katie Noble: front jacket, jacket flaps, back jacket bottom left and bottom center, 11, 81, 85, 107, 117, 189, 197; Thomas Lord: page 10, top;Tim Palin Creative: page 105; Thinkstock: 28, 32, 39, 47, 52, 59, 71, 79, 89, 99, 109, 114, 125, 129, 137,138, 151, 155, 159, 160, 165, 167, 169, 173, 175, 177, 179, 181, 185.

Printed in China

Contents

Introduction

Gelato, derived from the Latin word *gelātus*, meaning "frozen," is Italian ice cream. It is a dense, smooth, creamy, and flavorful frozen dessert that differs in three major ways from American ice cream.

- **Gelato is much lower in butterfat than American ice cream.** Most American ice cream has a butterfat content of 14 to 25 percent, while gelato's butterfat content generally ranges from 4 to 9 percent. Contrary to popular belief, less butterfat actually intensifies the flavor of gelato, providing a much more satisfying taste experience.

- **Gelato is denser than American ice cream.** American ice cream can have up to 50 percent or more air churned into it, compared to the 20 to 30 percent in gelato. Air can double the amount of ice cream produced in a single batch, increasing the yield but lowering the quality. The density of gelato not only creates a smoother and richer product but also ensures high quality in each batch produced. However, despite gelato's density, the low butterfat content helps maintain its lightness, creating the perfect combination of creamy and light.

- **Gelato is served at a warmer temperature than American ice cream.** Gelato is usually served at a temperature that is 10 to 15 degrees warmer than American ice cream. The warmer temperature reinforces the creamy texture and stunningly bold flavor of the gelato as it quickly melts in your mouth.

Anyone who has ever had real Italian gelato knows how life changing the experience can be. We're not talking about the "gelato" found in 70 percent of the shops worldwide that claim to make homemade Italian gelato. These shops may garner local accolades and start a consumer frenzy for gelato, but their product is not much different than the mix served at yogurt chains: it's premade and at times, chemically derived. It may look traditional. It may be beautifully displayed with bountiful colorful flavors garnished with whole pieces of fruit and chocolate, but often it's not real, traditional gelato.

In fact, gelato that is piled extravagantly high and conjures up images of carnival gaudiness should be avoided. True artisanal gelato cannot be mounded that high without melting, and neon colors should be fair warning that artificial coloring was used. Early on in my cooking career, I had the opportunity to learn the art of true gelato making in Italy, so I understand the difference between imitation and real gelato. Upon returning to the United States, I was disappointed with the products that many shops claimed to be gelato. So I set out to reestablish this disappearing craft and make pure Italian gelato one small batch at a time—or, as close to pure as I could get without being in Italy!

I've written this book to share my passion for gelato, teach the tradition of true Italian gelato making, and offer you more than fifty recipes to make at home. I've tested each recipe multiple times with my own home equipment and developed every one to be as simple to make as possible. Here you will find the type of ingredients you need and where to get them, the best equipment to use, and the step-by-step process of making gelato at home.

I will also tell you how we make gelato in the Morano Gelato laboratory as compared to artisanal laboratories throughout Italy. You will learn the system I have developed for combining the traditional gelato-making process in a laboratory with techniques you can apply at home to achieve similar results in flavor and texture.

The time for store-packaged ice cream and icy, artificially flavored gelato is over. Following these recipes will not only make you the most popular host of any dinner party but also the new neighborhood authority on authentic gelato.

Buon divertimento!
—Morgan Morano

My Path to Pure Italian Gelato

Often, I'm asked to speak to groups of students interested in learning more about starting a business, producing gelato, or both. When people hear that I started my gelato company without any business schooling or degree, they look surprised and perplexed. I have been well educated in both business and in making traditional Italian gelato—just not in the conventional way that people expect.

Business School 101

From a young age, I always told people I wanted my own food business, and I was given the tools and opportunities to develop my business skills. The tools came from my family. The opportunities came from my childhood on Fire Island.

I spent almost every summer up until age twenty-four in the small community of Ocean Beach on Fire Island. My father, with his two brothers and his parents, owned and operated a restaurant at the east end of Ocean Beach: Matthew's Seafood House. My father was a savvy entrepreneur, and growing up, I saw a compassionate and generous employer who was firm in his policies and his vision for the family business—fundamentals I've inherited from him and that I've learned are key to running a successful business.

My parents never gave my brother or me an allowance. Chores were an expected part of being a family member, and if I wanted money, I could make it in Ocean Beach. Selling shells and lemonade, delivering pizzas, carting luggage to weekend homes—these childhood "business ventures" allowed me to be creative and taught me how to interact with customers. I learned the art of selling at age six. To get people to buy our shells, my brother and I would shout, "Shells for sale!" and try to convince people walking past us that shells had many uses. Suggesting they use shells as ashtrays always seemed to work, so over time, we adjusted our strategy and narrowed our focus to passersby with cigarettes.

My father reinforced these lessons. When I'd come running into the restaurant disappointed with my $1.50 profit for the day, he would encourage my brother and me to try new strategies or sell better seashell products. He was my teacher, and Ocean Beach was the classroom—this was my business school.

My father passed away when I was eleven, but the lessons he taught me have stayed with me. When I got a little older, I began to work in the family restaurant. Matthew's taught me valuable lessons in business management and hard work. It was also there that I began to hone my passion for the culinary arts.

From Fire Island to Florence

In college, I decided to study abroad for a semester—and where better than Italy, the place of my family heritage. In Florence, my passion for food exploded. I was awed by the quality of food produced in Italy, and the attention to detail and presentation was like nothing I had ever seen in the States. When I returned home, I went to culinary school and then spent my time making money to fund more trips to Italy.

In the fall of 2007, during one of my trips, I wandered outside the city of Florence to look at an apartment listed for rent and found a Sicilian gelato and pastry shop. It was promoting Sicilian granita, so I tried their *Caffè* flavor with whipped cream. It was one of the most amazing desserts I had ever eaten! Craving another, I went back the next day on my lunch break, and that was when I first met Antonio Cafarelli, the owner and chef of this gelateria. When Antonio learned of my Sicilian heritage and culinary background, he offered to give me a production tour of his shop.

What struck me most about Antonio was his passion for quality and his high standards, both of which I shared. We decided to collaborate on a peanut butter–flavored gelato. He would teach me the process of making gelato if I would teach him how to make a New York–style cheesecake. I agreed, and an amazing partnership and friendship was born. Through Antonio, I gained a deep respect for what was quickly becoming a lost art. Few gelaterias were making traditional Italian gelato in Italy, and virtually no one was in America.

I began working full time for Antonio, and he took me under his wing, teaching me the science behind gelato making and showing me how true artisans worked. He taught me how to differentiate good gelato from premade gelato and showed me the artistic techniques of garnishing and displaying the finished product.

After my training, I was in charge of producing most of the gelato and pastries each day, along with cleaning and opening the shop and washing all the dishes. It was the hardest job I have ever had, but it brought a new meaning to my culinary career.

When I returned to United States, my work in Antonio's shop inspired the largest risk I have ever taken: starting my own gelato company. I moved in with my mother, who was living in New Hampshire, and in 2010, in a small New England town, Morano Gelato was born.

Morano Gelato Today

My philosophy at Morano Gelato is to serve the freshest and highest-quality gelato and sorbets made in the authentic Italian tradition. We spare no effort in making the best product possible, waking up early to start gelato production so we can finish in the afternoon and serve each flavor within hours of its extraction from the machine. Our gelato is an extremely fresh product, and we aim to sell out every evening. This ensures the highest-quality gelato for our customers.

Supporting the local agriculture and economy is important to me. I work with farms and businesses in the community to source important ingredients for the gelato and sorbet, and sometimes, they in turn inspire community-specific flavors. Even so, many of the ingredients come from Italy because of our ongoing commitment to making traditional and unique Italian flavors.

I've chosen to set my own path, combining traditional and modern production methods to make exceptional Italian gelato. Shortly after returning from Italy, I developed an uncommon process for producing gelato that combines Italian gelato methods and American ice cream–making techniques, which gives me control over the recipes, flavor profiles, and freshness, and ultimately results in a superior product.

Modern American ice cream production generally consists of individual recipes and bases cooked on a stove top, cooled, and then churned in an ice cream maker. American ice cream recipes involve a significant amount of whole milk, heavy cream, and egg yolks, which results in a product rich in fat and hard in consistency. Alternatively, Italian gelato production involves the use of one primary "white base" that is divided as needed per flavor. Ingredients are then added and blended in before the base is

churned. This white base usually consists of a combination of different types of sugars, milk, and cream and never contains egg yolks unless necessary for a particular flavor. Therefore, the base is much lighter in butterfat content and softer in consistency.

At Morano Gelato, we have combined the best of both processes. Unlike many artisanal *gelatai* ("makers"), we do not produce a single base. Instead, we use the Italian base ingredients to make bases individually tailored to each recipe. This is extremely important when making flavors that have different gradations of sweetness, and it allows me to control the exact percentages of each ingredient in the base. Here, and only here, is where I've combined American and Italian techniques. I employ this combination throughout the recipes in this book as well.

Ultimately, it is the tradition of making Italian gelato that continues to be my goal. This tradition involves respect for the history of the product and the art of creating it and decorating it for display. Italian food culture illustrates the old anecdote that anything really good takes time. Italians do not rush cooking. Their food is based on quality, time, and taste. Italian food is slow food.

Today, the tradition lies in the preservation of artisanal gelato and the culture surrounding it, including the flavors, the temperature at which the gelato is served, and the presentation. All of these elements have made gelato unique in the world of frozen desserts. Morano Gelato is and always will be dedicated to the true science and art of gelato making, especially as the company continues to grow and expand.

Home Gelato Machines, Tools, and Ingredients

To make delicious gelato and sorbet, you'll need the same equipment that is standard in any quality gelato shop, just on a smaller scale. The most important item, of course, is the gelato machine.

Gelato/Ice Cream Machine

Due to the popularity of making homemade ice cream, there are many home machines and manufacturers to choose from, with prices that range from $50 to $1,000 or more. The good news is you don't have to spend a fortune on the machine to produce a high-quality product. My recommendation is to not spend more than $300. There are many home machines in this price range that will work well with my recipes.

KEY FEATURES

The biggest difference you will find in home machines is how the canister freezes. There are two types: those with a detachable canister that needs to be prefrozen and those with a built-in compressor. The former is much more affordable and works just fine, while the latter is more expensive but saves time spent on prefreezing the canister.

Regardless of the brand and type you choose, I strongly recommend selecting a machine that has a removable bowl and paddle for ease of use and cleaning. Since you are working with a dairy product, it's very important that you clean and sanitize the machine and all its parts properly to inhibit mold or bacteria growth.

You will also find that some machines come with gelato-specific paddles that, according to the manufacturer, whip less air into the product. Although this may be true, I believe the difference is slight, and my recipes will work just as well in ice cream machines equipped with just one paddle.

Finally, be sure to purchase a machine with a capacity of at least 1.5 quarts (1.42 liters). Most of the recipes in this book yield between 1 quart (950 milliliters) and 1.5 quarts (1.42 liters) of gelato or sorbet. If you already own a 1-quart (950-milliliter) machine, you can simply scale the recipes back by multiplying each ingredient by .75.

RECOMMENDATIONS

The brands that have a strong reputation in the frozen dessert industry—both in America and in Italy—and that I personally think are best are Cuisinart and Lello. For the most authentic gelato experience, however, Lello would be my first choice.

Cuisinart's ICE models are great machines, and they come in a few different sizes and models. Furthermore, Cuisinart's ICE-100 Ice Cream and Gelato Maker has a compressor and two paddles, one for ice cream and one for gelato. The company's canister machines also work well and have consistently received great reviews.

Lello produces the machines that I have used for offsite events. In fact, Lello's Musso Pola was the first machine I bought back in 2010 to develop and test my recipes for the business. For this book, I tested all of the recipes on either a 1.5-quart (1.42-liter) Knox Gear Automatic Ice Cream Maker or a Lello Gelato Junior 4090. It takes the gelato a little longer to freeze than when using a prefrozen canister machine, but the results are a little softer—a plus when making gelato. I also appreciate not having to worry about prefreezing canisters prior to testing recipes back to back or when I want to make more than one flavor in a day.

Once you've chosen and purchased your home gelato machine, make sure to read all the manufacturer's guidelines for use. Freezing time may vary from machine to machine, so it's important that you keep an eye on the gelato the first few times you test one of my recipes in your machine. This will help prevent over- or under-churning the gelato and help you gauge how long you can expect future recipes to take.

Tools

Many of the tools used to make gelato and sorbet are items that you may already have in your kitchen. Be sure to assemble all your tools and materials before you begin to make the recipes.

HIGH-TEMPERATURE SPATULA

Silicone spatulas are best because they will not be affected by the hot temperature of the gelato base and they are easy to clean. Spatulas will also be needed to transfer the flavors and sorbets to bowls and in and out of the machine, along with swirling in mix-ins, or *variegati.*

STAINLESS-STEEL WHISK

A medium- to large-sized whisk is needed for all stages of the base's initial production prior to freezing as well as for making sorbet syrup.

KITCHEN SCALE

The scale you use should be durable and steady (any unevenness can result in incorrect measurements) and should be able to hold more than 4 pounds (1.8 kilograms). I strongly recommend a digital scale for ease of use. Waterproof scales are available if you're prone to spilling, but they generally cost more and are not usually worth the extra expense.

IMMERSION BLENDER

An immersion blender is a common tool in any gelato laboratory and is used to help incorporate and blend ingredients into the base. It's also needed for blending the ingredients in the sorbet recipes. A small home-kitchen immersion blender is fine, but I recommend one that has a detachable wand for easy cleaning.

SAUCEPAN

A 2.5-quart (2.36-liter) heavy-bottomed saucepan is needed to cook the base or syrup, although a 3- or 4-quart (2.84- or 3.78-liter) saucepan will also work. You want to have enough room to stir the base or syrup while it's cooking without having it spill over the sides.

BOWLS

I prefer glass bowls for prepping ingredients and for mixing, blending, and cooling the base or sorbet, but stainless-steel bowls will also work fine. It's most important that the bowls are heatproof and are the appropriate size. You may need a small or medium bowl for flavorings, yolks, or other measurements not immediately added to the base, and a large bowl for most of the measuring, mixing, and blending of the base.

SPOONS

Any spoon will work to test the taste and thickness of the base as well as the finished result out of the machine. You may also need a spoon to help add mix-ins, or variegati, to the gelato.

SPADE

The gelato spade is a simple tool that helps to separate authentic gelato from imitation. (When I first began selling gelato out of portable freezers at the farmer's market, Italophiles were more impressed that I scooped the gelato with an Italian spade than with the gelato itself!) A spade indicates that the gelato is the correct consistency, which is softer than ice cream that has to be served with an American scooper. The spade also acts as a tool with which the server can "work," or soften, the gelato to an even warmer temperature. Lastly, the spade allows the person scooping the gelato to chop up the ingredients within or on top of the flavor, such as the chocolate strips on *Stracciatella.*

STORAGE CONTAINERS

Glass or plastic containers with tight-fitting lids are best for storing your gelato in the freezer. Airtight containers are key to preventing freezer burn and ice crystallization. Just make sure the container you choose can hold at least 1.5 quarts (1.42 liters) of gelato or sorbet with a little room to spare for the lid. For long-term storage, wide, shallow containers are best because they offer greater surface area so the gelato softens more quickly and evenly.

PLASTIC WRAP, PARCHMENT PAPER, AND WAX PAPER

Plastic wrap is used to cover the top of the base while it's cooling in order to prevent a film from forming. It is also used to cover the top of the gelato after it has been removed from the gelato machine and placed in the appropriate storage container. Parchment or wax paper can be used instead of plastic wrap when covering the surface of the frozen gelato and, in fact, are best for presentation purposes because they help the gelato surface freeze more evenly than plastic wrap.

Ingredients and Sourcing

The better the quality of the ingredients you use in your recipes, the better the quality of your final product. It's a simple formula that always yields the best results. My gelato recipes use ingredients commonly found in gelato bases along with other ingredients that I've incorporated to help you achieve a professional-quality product at home. The majority of these ingredients should be easy to find in your local grocery store, although some uniquely Italian flavors may call for ingredients that are a little harder to find.

I've listed below the different types of ingredients, why I use them, and where you can find them. The structure of gelato depends on a balance between the liquids and solids, and the fats and sugars in each recipe. I've done my best to create easy-to-make balanced recipes that take little prep time and should work in any home kitchen without compromising the taste and texture you enjoy in commercial artisanal gelato and sorbets.

DAIRY

If possible, buy local dairy products to achieve the best flavor. Pasteurized whole milk and heavy cream are used in many of the recipes. Heavy cream with a butterfat content between 36 and 38 percent is preferred.

Nonfat dry milk powder helps give more structure to each flavor through the use of an additional solid ingredient. It contributes to a better mouth feel and texture, and it gives the gelato a stronger "milky" flavor. Milk powder can be found in the baking aisle of a supermarket.

For the two yogurt flavors, I've used powdered yogurt to achieve better textural results.

EGG

I prefer using large eggs from local farms when possible. I use yolks in certain flavors that call for a custard base or when further emulsification of the ingredients is necessary, particularly in those recipes using ground or powdered ingredients. Wherever you source your eggs, make sure they are the freshest and best quality you can buy.

SUGAR

Regular granulated sugar is used in all of the recipes along with light corn syrup. Both can be found in most grocery stores and contribute to the structure and texture of the gelato. Light corn syrup also helps reduce ice crystallization without overly sweetening the gelato. This is especially important when using a home machine to create a product low in butterfat, bold in flavor, and creamy in texture.

Corn syrup is not considered the same as high-fructose corn syrup (which is further processed) and using it shouldn't be a cause for alarm, particularly since only a small amount is called for in each recipe. Remember, sugar is sugar and gelato is a treat! There are natural substitutes for corn syrup available, but they do not achieve the same results; therefore, I strongly suggest sticking to corn syrup for these recipes to produce the best homemade gelato possible.

STARCH

Tapioca starch helps to thicken the gelato base and absorb water, further reducing ice crystallization. Tapioca starch is made from the cassava root and is commonly used as a natural thickener in various recipes. Furthermore, it's gluten free and growing in popularity in the United States. It should be available in the baking section of any supermarket or specialty food store, and is widely available from online sources. I used an organic tapioca starch for each recipe from Edward & Sons (www.edwardandsons.com).

NUT PASTES

For the pistachio and hazelnut recipes, I use ground-nut pastes. The ones made by Love'n Bake are easily available. I've chosen to incorporate nut pastes into the recipes for their ease, convenience, and taste. These pastes can be found online (www.americanalmond.com) and should be available in the baking aisle of supermarkets.

CHOCOLATE

Three different types of chocolate products are used in the recipes: an unsweetened cacao powder, a 60-percent dark chocolate, and a 100-percent dark chocolate. The higher the quality of chocolate, the better, and I recommend any of the following brands for all three types: Valrhona (www.valrhona-chocolate.com), Scharffen Berger (www.scharffenberger.com), Ghirardelli (www.ghirardelli.com), or Cacao Barry (www.cacao-barry.com). If you can't find a 60-percent dark chocolate, any type between 60 and 70 percent will work, but keep in mind that the higher the percentage of cacao, the more bitter your dark chocolate may be.

OTHER INGREDIENTS AND EXTRACTS

Each flavor calls for specific ingredients, many of which can be found in local grocery stores. Those flavors that are slightly more uncommon, such as Jasmine or *Cassata*, may require the purchase of ingredients online, in specialty stores, or in hard-to-find spots in local supermarkets. I've tried my best to create recipes that contain easy-to-find ingredients, but in order to replicate traditional Italian flavors, a few challenges are unavoidable.

In each recipe, I've listed the necessary ingredients along with the preferred brand or type, if applicable. If any additional work is required, such as cooking rice for Rice gelato, I've recommended trying your own recipe and offered shortcuts you can use if you're short on time. I always look for the highest-quality ingredients available even when taking shortcuts, and I hope you will, too, to ensure the best-tasting gelato possible.

FRESH FRUIT

As is common practice in artisanal gelato shops, using fresh fruit is always best unless otherwise specified. Most of the fruit-flavored recipes call for fresh fruit and no substitutes. The choice between organic or nonorganic is up to you, but the use of fresh, ripe, and flavorful fruit should not be compromised. Trust me. The results are worth it.

Step-by-Step Guide to Making Gelato and Sorbetto

Every gelato and sorbet flavor has its own unique ingredients, but the basic process for making gelato and sorbet at home is the same for all the recipes. Here are illustrated step-by-step instructions that take you through the basics of a gelato recipe and a sorbet recipe. The guide shows you what to do as well as how the mixture should look at various stages. Once you start making the actual gelato and sorbet flavors, you can refer back to the guide if you have any questions, making it as easy and simple as possible to produce mouthwatering gelato and sorbet right in your own kitchen. Below are a few general tips before you start.

You'll see that the ingredients for the recipes in this book are measured by weight, not volume. Don't be intimidated! Having never excelled in math, I understand that measuring by ounces and grams may seem foreign, but digital scales are very easy to use. More importantly, measuring by weight is the most accurate method for creating gelato that is consistently delicious each and every time you make it. Just make sure to always tare, or zero out, the scale before you put any ingredients into the bowl. (To zero out the scale, you simply push the zero key after you have put the item on the scale that you wish to deduct from the weight. That way, the weight of the measuring bowl won't get added to the weight of the ingredient itself.) Most digital scales measure in both ounces and grams. Although I've included both measurements in the recipes, I recommend measuring in grams because they are more accurate. This is the way I first measured the ingredients in each recipe, hence the grams are in whole numbers, which are easier to use.

Although most household freezers are set for 0 to 2 degrees Fahrenheit / −18 to −17 degrees Celsius, I recommend keeping your freezer between 2 and 4 degrees Fahrenheit / −17 and −16 degrees Celsius. My freezer is set to 2 degrees Fahrenheit / −17 degrees Celsius, and that is what I based the freezing time on for these recipes.

Our gelato at Morano Gelato is made fresh every morning to be eaten by customers that day. The same is true for the recipes in this book: for optimal flavor, I recommend that you enjoy the gelato (or sorbet) within 24 to 48 hours of preparation. From start to finish, these recipes should take no more than 12 hours, depending on the temperature of your freezer. If you're having a dinner party, make the gelato first thing in the morning so that it has time to harden all afternoon in the freezer. Or, you can prep the bases the night before, leave them to cool in the refrigerator overnight, and then churn the gelato first thing in the morning.

If you will not be ready to eat the gelato as soon as it is ready, you will need to take it out of the freezer and let it sit for the period of time indicated in each recipe before serving. The reason for this is that the ideal temperature for serving gelato or sorbet is 7 to 12 degrees Fahrenheit / −14 to −11 degrees Celsius. That is when they have the best texture and flavor. The freezer temperature is especially important with sorbet, which freezes much harder than gelato because of its high water content.

If you don't want to bother with letting the gelato sit out for 5 or more minutes after it's been in the freezer for an extensive period of time, set your freezer to a temperature between 7 and 10 degrees Fahrenheit / −14 to −12 degrees Celsius. Your gelato and sorbet will then always be at the perfect temperature for eating, and the freezer will still be well below the freezing point.

Before beginning to make gelato or sorbet, make sure you have all of the equipment and ingredients needed for the recipe. If you're using a gelato machine with a detachable canister, the canister will need to be prefrozen for a minimum of 12 to 24 hours. Make sure to follow the manufacturer's directions to ensure proper freezing.

Measuring Shortcut

There is a quick and easy measuring method that takes a bit of practice but will save you time and dishes once you get the hang of it. Start by placing a bowl large enough to hold the entire mixture on the scale and tare, or zero it out, to account for the weight of the container. Measure your first ingredient. Tare the scale again. It is now back to zero, and you can measure your second ingredient in the bowl already containing the first ingredient. You can remove the bowl from the scale when necessary to whisk ingredients together, then place it back on the scale, tare it again, and add the next ingredient. The tricky part of this method is making sure you add the ingredients slowly, particularly liquids. If you pour in too much liquid, it's pretty much impossible to remove it from the mix. You can practice by pouring water into a bowl on the scale to get a feel for how to get an accurate measurement without going over.

GELATO
Step by Step

1. Measure the dry ingredients for the base in a bowl, making sure to tare, or zero out the weight, once you put the bowl on the scale.

2. Remove the bowl from the scale and whisk to mix the dry ingredients together.

3. Measure the dairy and other liquid ingredients, add them to the dry ingredients, and whisk well to incorporate the dry ingredients into the liquid.

4. (a) Follow by adding the corn syrup and any other ingredients the recipe calls for, and either whisk or blend them together with an immersion blender. (b) If using an immersion blender, the ingredients should be fully blended into the base while incorporating the least amount of air possible. To do this, place the immersion blender stick into the bowl and turn it on for a few seconds, rotating the stick, then turn it off. Move the blender stick to a new position in the base and turn it on to blend and rotate, then off. Repeat as needed, each time moving the blender stick to a new position. This allows you to blend the ingredients without incorporating too much air into the base—and it also helps prevent a huge mess! Finely chopping fruit, nuts, and other ingredients will help reduce blender time.

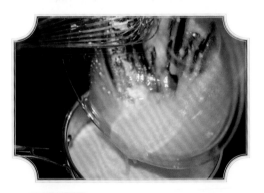

5. Empty the base into a 2.5-quart / 2.36-liter saucepan, using the whisk or a spatula to scrape the sides of the bowl.

6. Place the saucepan on the stove, turn the heat to medium-high, and begin to cook, whisking continuously to prevent any clumping or burning of the ingredients. You can whisk slowly in the beginning, but you should pick up speed as the base begins to steam and then thicken.

7. As the base steams and thickens, its appearance will change noticeably. It will no longer look thin or foamy but will have a nice sheen to it. The whisk will move more slowly through the thickening base—and in an instant, the base will be fully thickened. This should happen right before it begins to boil. Upon thickening, just to be sure the starch is fully activated, I recommend cooking the base 15 seconds longer while whisking intensely to prevent any burning. Once finished, remove the base immediately from the heat. You can check the thickness of the base with a "spoon test." Dip a stainless-steel spoon into the cooked base. If the base has thickened properly, it should coat the back of the spoon generously enough so that if you run your finger across it, the base will continue to stick to the spoon on either side of the clean line left by your finger.

8. Pour the base into a glass or other heatproof bowl and cover it immediately with plastic wrap to prevent a skin from forming on the top as it cools. Some recipes may call for ingredients to be whisked in before covering and cooling. If that is case, make sure to do it quickly, before a skin can start to form. Allow the base to cool for 30 to 45 minutes and then place it in your refrigerator for a minimum of 4 hours and a maximum of 12 hours to cool completely. Although I prefer cooling the base in a refrigerator, you can speed up the process by cooling it in an ice bath. You will want to submerge the bowl at least halfway into the bath to help cool it down, but be careful that no ice or water gets into the base. Make sure to refresh the ice as necessary. When using this method, the base should be fully cooled within 30 to 45 minutes.

9. Once the base has cooled completely, it will thicken even further, and this should be evident in its appearance. Additionally, certain ingredients will absorb some of the base liquid and their visibility will be greater. With the help of a spatula, carefully pour the base into the bowl of your gelato machine and churn according to the manufacturer's directions. Each recipe should take between 30 and 55 minutes to churn. If you decide to halve the recipe, the churning/freezing time of the batch should be less.

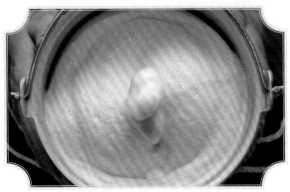

10. The gelato is ready when it has expanded and thickened to a point where the base is visibly frozen and has begun pulling away from the sides of the canister. The gelato will begin to spiral around the paddle in a thick mass. It's important to neither over-churn the gelato nor pull it out too early. The machine paddle will begin to move much more slowly through the base as it thickens, and you should listen for this sound to help determine if the base is ready. It should be semi-firm when you're extracting it from the machine but still easy enough to scoop with a spatula into a storage container.

11. Any storage container will work, plastic or glass, as long as it has a tight-fitting lid to keep the air out. Exposure to the freezer air may result in ice crystallization or freezer burn on the surface of the gelato, so make sure to use high-quality storage containers.

Once the gelato has been scooped into the storage container, cover the surface with plastic wrap or parchment paper, seal the container with the airtight lid, and then put it in your freezer for 4 to 5 hours, or until the gelato has hardened further but is still soft enough to scoop.

SORBETTO
Step by Step

Sorbet Syrup

1. Measure the sugar and starch in a bowl, making sure to tare, or zero out the weight, once you put the bowl on the scale.

2. Add the water and corn syrup and whisk well to incorporate all of the dry ingredients into the liquid.

3. Pour the syrup into a 2.5-quart / 2.36-liter saucepan on medium-high heat and begin to cook, whisking continuously to prevent burning. The whisking can be slower in the beginning but should pick up speed as the syrup begins to steam. The syrup will thicken slightly just before boiling, about 12 to 15 minutes. Once finished, remove the syrup immediately from the heat and pour into a heatproof bowl.

4. Allow the uncovered syrup to cool at room temperature for about 30 to 45 minutes. Then cover the container with plastic wrap and place the syrup in the refrigerator to chill for a minimum of 4 hours. Once the syrup has fully cooled, use immediately or transfer to a storage container with a tight-fitting lid. The syrup can be stored in the refrigerator for up to 4 days.

Sorbetto

1. Measure the prepared fruit in a bowl. Add the syrup, water, and other ingredients. The syrup must be whisked well before using, as the starch will settle when the syrup is stored in the refrigerator.

2. Blend the mixture with an immersion blender. Each piece of fruit should be fully blended into the syrup and water while incorporating the least amount of air possible. To do this, place the immersion blender stick into the bowl and turn it on for a few seconds to blend, then off. Place it on a new piece of fruit and turn it on to blend, then off, and so on. This allows you to blend each piece of fruit without incorporating too much air into the sorbet base—and it also helps prevent a huge mess! Finely chopping the fruit before adding it to the mixture will also reduce the amount of blending needed.

3. Carefully pour the sorbet into the bowl of your gelato machine, using a spatula to ensure you get all the ingredients into the machine. Churn according to the manufacturer's directions. Each recipe should take between 30 to 55 minutes to churn. If you decide to halve the recipe, the freezing/churning time for the batch should be less. The sorbet is ready when it has expanded and thickened to a point where it is visibly frozen and has begun pulling away from the sides of the canister. It's important not to over-churn the sorbet or it will become icy, however, it's also important not to pull it too early or you could get the same icy result. The machine paddle will begin to move much more slowly through the sorbet as it thickens, and you should listen for this sound to help determine if the sorbet is ready. It should be semi-firm when you're taking it out of the machine, but still easy enough to scoop with a spatula into a storage container.

4. Once the sorbet is ready, transfer it to a storage container and cover the surface of the sorbet with plastic wrap or parchment paper. Any storage container will work, plastic or glass, as long as it has an airtight lid. Exposure to the freezer air may result in ice crystallization or freezer burn on the surface of the sorbet, so make sure to use good-quality storage containers. Place the sorbet in your freezer for 4 to 5 hours or until the sorbet has hardened further but is still soft enough to scoop.

LE BASI
The Basics

FIOR DI LATTE
Sweet Milk

Similar to vanilla, Fior di Latte, literally translated as "flower of milk," is Italy's most basic flavor. Though seemingly humble, it's one of the most important flavors in any artisanal gelato shop. Fior di Latte is used as the base for many other flavors, and it also serves as a standard used by gelato enthusiasts and traditionalists to evaluate just how authentic and pure a shop's gelato is.

For the best flavor, Fior di Latte gelato should be made with the freshest milk available. At Morano Gelato, we use local dairy products from nearby dairy farms that provide us with high-quality milk and cream for all of our gelato.

Fior di Latte gelato should be creamy, light, and sweet, and should retain the flavor of the milk itself. Eating this gelato should remind you of drinking a smooth, cold glass of milk on a hot day . . . but better. Fior di Latte can be paired with any gelato flavor or enjoyed on its own.

Tapioca Starch

Tapioca starch is a thickening agent that comes from the root of the cassava plant. In the United States, cassava flour is the same as tapioca starch. A fine white powder, tapioca starch is naturally gluten free, and adds structure without the grittiness of some thickeners.

Ingredients

2 ounces / 56 grams milk powder

6.35 ounces / 180 grams granulated sugar

0.7 ounce / 20 grams tapioca starch

6.75 ounces / 192 grams heavy cream

24.15 ounces / 685 grams whole milk

0.9 ounce / 25 grams light corn syrup

Yield: About 1.5 quarts / 1.42 liters

Prepare

1. Mix the milk powder, sugar, and tapioca starch in a bowl.
2. Add the heavy cream and whole milk and whisk well to incorporate all of the dry ingredients into the liquid.
3. Whisk in the corn syrup.

Cook

4. Pour the mixture into a 2.5-quart / 2.36-liter saucepan, using a spatula to scrape the sides of the bowl. Place the saucepan on medium-high heat and cook, whisking continuously to prevent any burning or clumping. Whisk slowly in the beginning and increase speed as the mixture gets warmer and begins to steam and thicken. It should thicken without boiling after 8 to 12 minutes on the heat; watch carefully so it doesn't burn. Once the mixture has thickened enough to coat the back of a spoon, continue cooking 15 seconds longer, whisking vigorously. Then immediately remove from the heat.

Freeze

5. Pour the mixture into a clean glass or stainless-steel bowl and lay plastic wrap directly on the surface to prevent a skin from forming on top. Allow the mixture to sit 30 to 45 minutes, until no longer hot. Then place it in the refrigerator to cool completely, about 4 hours. If the mixture needs to be used right away, submerge most of the bowl in an ice bath and let it sit 30 to 40 minutes, refreshing the ice as necessary.

6. Once the mixture has cooled completely and thickened further, pour it into the bowl of the gelato machine and churn the gelato according to the manufacturer's directions. The gelato will expand and should spin until it's thick and creamy but still soft enough to scoop into a storage container, about 30 to 55 minutes.

7. Using a rubber spatula, scoop the gelato into a storage container.

8. Press a piece of plastic wrap or parchment paper directly on the surface of the gelato, seal the container with an airtight lid, and put it in the freezer.

9. Freeze at least 4 to 5 hours. When ready, the gelato should be firm enough to scoop but soft and creamy in texture.

Serve

10. Enjoy the fresh gelato as soon as possible. If using after 1 day, allow 7 to 10 minutes for the gelato to soften outside of the freezer before eating.

CREMA ALL'UOVO
Custard

Custard is a simple but important flavor in any gelato shop. The popular addition of Marsala wine from Sicily to the egg-yolk base rounds out the flavor and gives the gelato a new dimension of flavor and sweetness.

Crema all'Uovo can be paired with almost any flavor, but it's particularly nice with a chocolate or fruit flavor. I recommend a sweet Marsala for this recipe, but any kind will work.

Ingredients

1.6 ounces / 46 grams milk powder

7.6 ounces / 215 grams granulated sugar

1 pinch kosher salt

0.7 ounce / 20 grams tapioca starch

8.8 ounces / 250 grams heavy cream

21.15 ounces / 600 grams whole milk

0.35 ounce / 10 grams sweet
    Marsala wine

1.15 ounces / 33 grams light corn syrup

4 egg yolks

Yield: About 1.5 quarts / 1.42 liters

Prepare

1. Mix the milk powder, sugar, salt, and tapioca starch in a bowl.
2. Add the heavy cream, whole milk, and Marsala wine and whisk well to incorporate all of the dry ingredients into the liquid.
3. Whisk in the corn syrup and egg yolks.

Cook

4. Pour the mixture into a 2.5-quart / 2.36-liter saucepan, using a spatula to scrape the sides of the bowl. Place the saucepan on medium-high heat and cook, whisking continuously to prevent any burning or clumping. Whisk slowly in the beginning and increase speed as the mixture gets warmer and begins to steam and thicken. It should thicken without boiling after 8 to 12 minutes on the heat; watch carefully so it doesn't burn. Once the mixture has thickened enough to coat the back of a spoon, continue cooking 15 seconds longer, whisking vigorously. Then immediately remove from the heat.

Freeze

5. Pour the mixture into a clean glass or stainless-steel bowl and lay plastic wrap directly on the surface to prevent a skin from forming on top. Allow the mixture to sit 30 to 45 minutes, until no longer hot. Then place it in the refrigerator to cool completely, about 4 hours. If the mixture needs to be used right away, submerge most of the bowl in an ice bath and let it sit 30 to 40 minutes, refreshing the ice as necessary.
6. Once the mixture has cooled completely and thickened further, pour it into the bowl of the gelato machine and churn the gelato according to the manufacturer's directions. The gelato will expand and should spin until it's thick and creamy but still soft enough to scoop into a storage container, about 30 to 55 minutes.
7. Using a rubber spatula, scoop the gelato into a storage container.
8. Press a piece of plastic wrap or parchment paper directly on the surface of the gelato, seal the container with an airtight lid, and put it in the freezer.
9. Freeze at least 4 to 5 hours. When ready, the gelato should be firm enough to scoop but soft and creamy in texture.

Serve

10. Enjoy the fresh gelato as soon as possible. If using after 1 day, allow 7 to 10 minutes for the gelato to soften outside of the freezer before eating.

LO YOGURT
Yogurt

Lo Yogurt is a universal flavor found in any gelato shop. It's often placed in the display case next to other classics, such as Fior di Latte (page 30) and Crema all'Uovo (page 34).

Yogurt gelato may not be as nutritious as frozen yogurt, but it makes up for that tenfold in flavor. I've never been a fan of store-bought frozen yogurt, but when I first tasted Yogurt gelato, the consistency and tang immediately won me over. It doesn't taste icy with a faint yogurt flavor. Instead, it is creamy, sweet, and full of flavor—just as you would imagine a yogurt-flavored dessert should be. Some customers tell me that, when paired with a fruit flavor, Yogurt gelato creates the ultimate cheesecake-tasting frozen dessert.

Yogurt gelato is a great flavor to pair with any sliced fruit or berries. I also recommend blending it into a smoothie or simply pairing it with any one of my fruit sorbet recipes for a frozen combination that's tangy, sweet, and creamy. For a fun twist, try heating up a little Nutella and drizzling it over the top of this gelato. The flavor will echo another popular gelato we make in the shop, Yogurt e Nutella, and shouldn't be missed!

Ingredients

1.25 ounces / 35 grams milk powder

6.7 ounces / 190 grams granulated sugar

0.7 ounce / 20 grams tapioca starch

6.75 ounces / 192 grams heavy cream

24.15 ounces / 685 grams whole milk

1.27 ounces / 36 grams light corn syrup

1.05 ounces / 30 grams yogurt powder

0.1 ounce / 3 grams fresh-squeezed
    lemon juice

Blueberries, or other fruit for garnish (optional)

Yield: About 1.5 quarts / 1.42 liters

Prepare

1. Mix the milk powder, sugar, and tapioca starch in a bowl.
2. Add the heavy cream and whole milk and whisk well to incorporate all of the dry ingredients into the liquid.
3. Whisk in the corn syrup.

Cook

4. Pour the mixture into a 2.5-quart / 2.36-liter saucepan, using a spatula to scrape the sides of the bowl. Place the saucepan on medium-high heat and cook, whisking continuously to prevent any burning or clumping. Whisk slowly in the beginning and increase speed as the mixture gets warmer and begins to steam and thicken. It should thicken without boiling after 8 to 12 minutes on the heat; watch carefully so it doesn't burn. Once the mixture has thickened enough to coat the back of a spoon, continue cooking 15 seconds longer, whisking vigorously. Then immediately remove from the heat.

Freeze

5. Pour the mixture into a clean glass or stainless-steel bowl. Add the yogurt powder to the hot base by sifting it through a fine mesh sieve to help break up any lumps. Whisk well to incorporate the yogurt powder, breaking up any remaining lumps.

6. Lay plastic wrap directly on the surface to prevent a skin from forming on top. Allow the mixture to sit 30 to 45 minutes until no longer hot. Then place it in the refrigerator to cool completely, about 4 hours. If the mixture needs to be used right away, submerge most of the bowl in an ice bath and let it sit 30 to 40 minutes, refreshing the ice as necessary.

7. Once the mixture has cooled completely and thickened further, lightly whisk in the lemon juice.

8. Pour the mixture into the bowl of the gelato machine and churn the gelato according to the manufacturer's directions. The gelato will expand and should spin until it's thick and creamy but still soft enough to scoop into a storage container, about 30 to 55 minutes.

9. Using a rubber spatula, scoop the gelato into a storage container.

10. Press a piece of plastic wrap or parchment paper directly on the surface of the gelato, seal the container with an airtight lid, and put it in the freezer.

11. Freeze at least 4 to 5 hours. When ready, the gelato should be firm enough to scoop but soft and creamy in texture.

Serve

12. Enjoy the fresh gelato as soon as possible. If using after 1 day, allow 8 to 10 minutes for the gelato to soften outside of the freezer before eating. Garnish with blueberries, if desired.

Yogurt Powder

Powdered yogurt is uncommon in yogurt ice cream recipes, but I prefer using it to help give the yogurt flavor the tang it needs without taking away from the creaminess of the gelato. After all, it is yogurt gelato, not frozen yogurt. Yogurt powder can be found in specialty food shops or natural foods stores. It can also be purchased online. I tested the recipes in this book with powdered yogurt made by Hoosier Hill Farm (www.hoosierhillfarm.com).

CAFFÈ
Italian Espresso

Espresso bars are a significant part of Italian culture. They are everywhere, and Italians take their espresso very seriously. Almost all are experts at tasting the difference between good and bad espresso, and I have many friends who drink up to eight shots a day! Like making gelato, the romance of making Italian espresso resonated with me during my first trip to Italy. It's only right that an espresso gelato should be made with the same attention to detail as Italian baristas give their espresso.

I love both my espresso and coffee light and sweet, and that's exactly how this gelato tastes. At Morano Gelato, we've begun to serve Illy's espresso blend, a well-balanced espresso enjoyed throughout Italy. The result is a balanced, sweet, and strong flavor that produces thoughts of freshly pulled espresso shots with the perfect crema, or foam, on top.

Italian Espresso gelato is a great dessert to serve at the end of a meal. Paired with Dark Chocolate gelato (page 48), it's irresistible. Or, you can try adding a small scoop to your morning coffee for an indulgent way to start the day. Italian Espresso gelato also makes a great frappé when blended with milk (page 51)—the perfect afternoon "pick-me-up."

Ingredients

2 ounces / 56 grams milk powder

6.35 ounces / 180 grams granulated sugar

0.15 ounce / 4 grams espresso grounds

0.7 ounce / 20 grams tapioca starch

7.6 ounces / 215 grams heavy cream

21.15 ounces / 600 grams whole milk

1.25 ounces / 35 grams light corn syrup

3 ounces / 85 grams brewed and cooled espresso (just over 1 shot)

1 egg yolk

Yield: About 1.5 quarts / 1.42 liters

Prepare

1. Mix the milk powder, sugar, espresso grounds, and tapioca starch in a bowl.
2. Add the heavy cream and whole milk and whisk well to incorporate all of the dry ingredients into the liquid.
3. Whisk in the corn syrup, espresso, and egg yolk.

Cook

4. Pour the mixture into a 2.5-quart / 2.36-liter saucepan, using a spatula to scrape the sides of the bowl. Place the saucepan on medium-high heat and cook, whisking continuously to prevent any burning or clumping. Whisk slowly in the beginning and increase speed as the mixture gets warmer and begins to steam and thicken. It should thicken without boiling after 8 to 12 minutes on the heat; watch carefully so it doesn't burn. Once the mixture has thickened enough to coat the back of a spoon, continue cooking 15 seconds longer, whisking vigorously. Then immediately remove from the heat.

Freeze

5. Pour the mixture into a clean glass or stainless-steel bowl and lay plastic wrap directly on the surface to prevent a skin from forming on top. Allow the mixture to sit 30 to 45 minutes, until no longer hot. Then place it in the refrigerator to cool completely, about 4 hours. If the mixture needs to be used right away, submerge most of the bowl in an ice bath and let it sit 30 to 40 minutes, refreshing the ice as necessary.

6. Once the mixture has cooled completely and thickened further, pour it into the bowl of the gelato machine and churn the gelato according to the manufacturer's directions. The gelato will expand and should spin until it's thick and creamy but still soft enough to scoop into a storage container, about 30 to 55 minutes.

7. Using a rubber spatula, scoop the gelato into a storage container.

8. Press a piece of plastic wrap or parchment paper directly on the surface of the gelato, seal the container with an airtight lid, and put it in the freezer.

9. Freeze at least 4 to 5 hours. When ready, the gelato should be firm enough to scoop but soft and creamy in texture.

Serve

10. Enjoy the fresh gelato as soon as possible. If using after 1 day, allow 7 to 10 minutes for the gelato to soften outside of the freezer before eating.

Espresso

At Morano Gelato, we use an Illy espresso blend for our Caffè gelato, but any espresso or strong coffee will work in this recipe. Just make sure it's bold in flavor and has a taste you enjoy. I also add espresso grounds to this gelato for a little more flavor, texture, and contrast to the color of the base.

STRACCIATELLA
Chocolate Chip

Named for the *straccia*, "strips" or "shreds" of chocolate, in the gelato, Italy's version of chocolate chip is much more decorative in appearance than its American ice cream counterpart. The pieces of chocolate that speckle this gelato have been previously melted, causing them to dissolve more quickly in the mouth. Additional spoonfuls of melted chocolate drizzled all over the top combine with the milky flavor and creamy texture of the base to create a much-favored flavor. Stracciatella is one of the few flavors that almost always sells out daily at Morano Gelato, and it's easy to understand why.

Any dark chocolate (60 to 70 percent cacao) will work for the chocolate-chip base, but my preference is 60 percent cacao. Although the base is simple, an extra step is required to melt and add the chocolate after the gelato has finished freezing. Don't be tempted to add more chocolate to the recipe because it will change the consistency of the gelato. A little extra chocolate on top enhances the presentation as well as the flavor of the gelato, and this is how it is served in Italy. Stracciatella gelato goes with just about any dessert or gelato flavor, but when blended with Menta gelato (page 90), it creates an irresistible frappé (page 51).

Ingredients

2 ounces / 56 grams milk powder

6.35 ounces / 180 grams granulated sugar

0.7 ounce / 20 grams tapioca starch

6.75 ounces / 192 grams heavy cream

24.15 ounces / 685 grams whole milk

0.95 ounce / 27 grams light corn syrup

5.3 ounces / 150 grams 60% to 70% dark chocolate, chopped into small pieces

Yield: About 1.5 quarts / 1.42 liters

Prepare

1. Mix the milk powder, sugar, and tapioca starch in a bowl.
2. Add the heavy cream and whole milk and whisk well to incorporate all of the dry ingredients into the liquid.
3. Whisk in the corn syrup.

Cook

4. Pour the mixture into a 2.5-quart / 2.36-liter saucepan, using a spatula to scrape the sides of the bowl. Place the saucepan on medium-high heat and cook, whisking continuously to prevent any burning or clumping. Whisk slowly in the beginning and increase speed as the mixture gets warmer and begins to steam and thicken. It should thicken without boiling after 8 to 12 minutes on the heat; watch carefully so it doesn't burn. Once the mixture has thickened enough to coat the back of a spoon, continue cooking 15 seconds longer, whisking vigorously. Then immediately remove from the heat.

Freeze

5. Pour the mixture into a clean glass or stainless-steel bowl and lay plastic wrap directly on the surface to prevent a skin from forming on top. Allow the mixture to sit 30 to 45 minutes until no longer hot. Then place it in the refrigerator to cool completely, about 4 hours. If the mixture needs to be used right away, submerge most of the bowl in an ice bath and let it sit 30 to 40 minutes, refreshing the ice as necessary.
6. Once the mixture has cooled completely and thickened further, pour it into the bowl of the gelato machine and churn the gelato according to the manufacturer's directions. The gelato will expand and should spin until it's thick and creamy but still soft enough to scoop into a storage container, about 30 to 55 minutes.

7. Using a rubber spatula, scoop the gelato into a storage container. Place the uncovered container immediately in the freezer and begin prepping the chocolate chip base.

Prepare the Chocolate

8. Fill a small saucepan a quarter of the way with water and bring to a simmer over medium heat. The water should remain at a simmer. Place the chocolate in a heatproof glass bowl over the saucepan to create a double boiler. The bowl should fit snugly on top of the saucepan, but the bottom of the bowl should not touch the water. The steam from the simmering water will melt the chocolate. Using a heatproof spatula, stir the chocolate from time to time to ensure even melting.

9. Once the chocolate is fully melted and liquid, turn off the heat and carefully remove the bowl from the saucepan. Allow the chocolate to cool slightly for 2 minutes. Remove the gelato from the freezer. It's important to work very quickly as the gelato should not melt much during this process. Using a tablespoon, begin drizzling the melted chocolate into the gelato and gently swirl it in with a spatula. Save a small amount of chocolate to drizzle on top before serving. The chocolate should freeze upon contact with the gelato. Make sure to incorporate the chocolate into the gelato at the bottom of the container so that little pieces of chocolate can be seen throughout the gelato. Do not take more than 3 minutes to add in the chocolate or the gelato will begin to melt.

10. Press a piece of plastic wrap or parchment paper directly on the surface of the gelato, seal the storage container with an airtight lid, and put it in the freezer.

11. Freeze at least 4 to 5 hours. When ready, the gelato should be firm enough to scoop but soft and creamy in texture. Remove the gelato from the freezer a few minutes before serving.

Serve

12. Reheat the chocolate set aside for garnish either over the pot of simmering water used before or in the microwave on low, being careful that it doesn't burn. Drizzle chocolate decoratively on top of the gelato. Put the gelato back in the freezer for 5 more minutes to allow the chocolate to harden before serving.

13. Enjoy the fresh gelato as soon as possible. If using after 1 day, allow 8 to 10 minutes for the gelato to soften outside of the freezer before eating.

CIOCCOLATO FONDENTE
Dark Chocolate

Many gelato shops will choose to distinguish between the different types of chocolate used, such as dark, milk, white, or even extra-dark (*nero fondente*). Some artisanal shops will even specify the brand of chocolate used in their creations, particularly if it's a highly regarded producer. No matter what chocolate is used, there's no doubt that a strongly flavored, smooth, and creamy chocolate gelato indicates a gelato chef who knows his or her trade well.

This gelato isn't as dark as our own dark chocolate at Morano Gelato (we offer a milk-chocolate flavor as well), but it has a nice depth of flavor that is rich and sweet and sure to please any chocolate lover. Two types of chocolate are used for this recipe in addition to the cacao powder. (There is a difference between cacao and cocoa powder, see page 50, but either will work.) Choose the highest-quality chocolate and cacao powder available, keeping in mind that the better and purer the chocolate, the better the gelato will taste.

Cioccolato Fondente gelato stands alone because of its strong flavor, but chocoholics will find it delicious paired with just about any other gelato. Or you can enjoy it as I always have—blended with whole milk as a frappé (page 51) and topped with whipped cream.

Ingredients

1.25 ounces / 35 grams milk powder

7.95 ounces / 225 grams granulated sugar

2 pinches kosher salt

1.05 ounces / 30 grams cacao powder

0.7 ounce / 20 grams tapioca starch

6.75 ounces / 192 grams heavy cream

24.15 ounces / 685 grams whole milk

1.4 ounces / 40 grams light corn syrup

2 egg yolks

0.9 ounce / 25 grams 100% dark chocolate, finely chopped

1.4 ounces / 40 grams 60% to 70% dark chocolate, finely chopped

Yield: About 1.5 quarts / 1.42 liters

Prepare

1. Mix the milk powder, sugar, salt, cacao powder, and tapioca starch in a bowl.
2. Add the heavy cream and whole milk and whisk well to incorporate all of the dry ingredients into the liquid.
3. Whisk in the corn syrup and egg yolks.
4. Put both kinds of dark chocolate into a separate glass or heatproof bowl that's large enough to hold the entire base once it has finished cooking. Set aside and begin cooking the base.

Cacao vs. Cocoa

Cacao powder is raw chocolate in its purest form. It will contribute a bolder chocolate flavor, which is why I prefer it. Generally, cocoa powder has additives, and sometimes even sweeteners, that affect the flavor of the powder.

Natural and unsweetened cocoa powder is a close second to cacao powder and is best if cacao powder is not available.

Cook

5. Pour the mixture into a 2.5-quart / 2.36-liter saucepan, using a spatula to scrape the sides of the bowl. Place the saucepan on medium-high heat and cook, whisking continuously to prevent any burning or clumping. Whisk slowly in the beginning and increase speed as the mixture gets warmer and begins to steam and thicken. It should thicken without boiling after 8 to 12 minutes on the heat; watch carefully so it doesn't burn. Once the mixture has thickened enough to coat the back of a spoon, continue cooking 15 seconds longer, whisking vigorously. Then immediately remove from the heat.

Freeze

6. Pour half of the hot base into the bowl containing the chocolate and whisk to allow the chocolate to melt and incorporate into the mixture. Then whisk in the rest of the hot base, making sure all of the chocolate is fully melted and mixed in.

7. Lay plastic wrap directly on the surface to prevent a skin from forming on top. Allow the mixture to sit 30 to 45 minutes, until no longer hot. Then place it in the refrigerator to cool completely, about 4 hours. If the mixture needs to be used right away, submerge most of the bowl in an ice bath and let it sit 30 to 40 minutes, refreshing the ice as necessary.

8. Once the mixture has cooled completely and thickened further, pour it into the bowl of the gelato machine and churn the gelato according to the manufacturer's directions. The gelato will expand and should spin until it's thick and creamy but still soft enough to scoop into a storage container, about 30 to 55 minutes.

9. Using a rubber spatula, scoop the gelato into a storage container.

10. Press a piece of plastic wrap or parchment paper directly on the surface of the gelato, seal the container with an airtight lid, and put it in the freezer.

11. Freeze at least 4 to 5 hours. When ready, the gelato should be firm enough to scoop but soft and creamy in texture.

Serve

12. Enjoy the fresh gelato as soon as possible. If using after 1 day, allow 10 to 15 minutes for the gelato to soften outside of the freezer before eating.

Frappé

You can use this recipe to make a chocolate or any other flavor of frappé. Any type of milk works, but for the best results, I recommend using whole milk. If you're using two different kinds of gelato, just divide the gelato measurement by half so that equal parts of each flavor are incorporated into the frappé. An Italian frappé is much lighter and thinner than an American milkshake but still flavorful. If you prefer a thicker version, you're welcome to add more gelato to achieve the desired consistency.

5.3 ounces / 150 grams gelato
7 ounces / 200 grams whole milk

Yield: 12 ounces / 355 milliliters

Place gelato and milk into a blender and blend until all of the gelato is incorporated into the milk, and the mixture is smooth and creamy. Top with whipped cream, if desired. Enjoy!

I CLASSICI
The Classics

YOGURT GRECO
Greek Yogurt

Yogurt Greco gelato does not contain the typical thick Greek yogurt but is rather an enhanced variation of the classic yogurt flavor. The base recipe uses a little yogurt powder and lemon juice to give the gelato its typical yogurt flavor, but for those who want something more, adds chopped walnuts, honey, and cinnamon. The cinnamon spice and sweet honey complement one another to deliver a delicious and unique flavor.

Ingredients

1.25 ounces / 35 grams milk powder

6.35 ounces / 180 grams granulated sugar

1 pinch ground cinnamon

0.7 ounce / 20 grams tapioca starch

6.75 ounces / 192 grams heavy cream

24.15 ounces / 685 grams whole milk

1.41 ounces / 40 grams light corn syrup

1.06 ounces / 30 grams honey

1.25 ounces / 35 grams walnuts, chopped

1.05 ounces / 30 grams yogurt powder

0.1 ounce / 3 grams fresh-squeezed lemon juice

Yield: About 1.5 quarts / 1.42 liters

Prepare

1. Mix the milk powder, sugar, cinnamon, and tapioca starch in a bowl.

2. Add the heavy cream and whole milk and whisk well to incorporate all of the dry ingredients into the liquid.

3. Whisk in the corn syrup, honey, and walnuts. (If the honey is too thick, warm it a little to make it fluid enough to pour.)

Cook

4. Pour the mixture into a 2.5-quart / 2.36-liter saucepan, using a spatula to scrape the sides of the bowl. Place the saucepan on medium-high heat and cook, whisking continuously to prevent any burning or clumping. Whisk slowly in the beginning and increase speed as the mixture gets warmer and begins to steam and thicken. It should thicken without boiling after 8 to 12 minutes on the heat; watch carefully so it doesn't burn. Once the mixture has thickened enough to coat the back of a spoon, continue cooking 15 seconds longer, whisking vigorously. Then immediately remove from the heat.

Freeze

5. Pour the mixture into a clean glass or stainless-steel bowl. Add the yogurt powder to the hot base by sifting it through a fine mesh sieve to help break up any lumps. Whisk well to incorporate the yogurt powder, breaking up any remaining lumps.

6. Lay plastic wrap directly on the surface to prevent a skin from forming on top. Allow the mixture to sit 30 to 45 minutes until no longer hot. Then place it in the refrigerator to cool completely, about 4 hours. If the mixture needs to be used right away, submerge most of the bowl in an ice bath and let it sit 30 to 40 minutes, refreshing the ice as necessary.

7. Once the mixture has cooled completely and thickened further, lightly whisk in the lemon juice.

8. Pour the mixture into the bowl of the gelato machine and churn the gelato according to the manufacturer's directions. The gelato will expand and should spin until it's thick and creamy but still soft enough to scoop into a storage container, about 30 to 55 minutes.

9. Using a rubber spatula, scoop the gelato into a storage container.

10. Press a piece of plastic wrap or parchment paper directly on the surface of the gelato, seal the container with an airtight lid, and put it in the freezer.

11. Freeze at least 4 to 5 hours. When ready, the gelato should be firm enough to scoop but soft and creamy in texture.

Serve

12. Enjoy the fresh gelato as soon as possible. If using after 1 day, allow 8 to 12 minutes for the gelato to soften outside of the freezer before eating.

CILIEGIA
Cherry

This recipe is made with fresh cherries. While any variety that is in season will work, sour cherries or bing cherries are the two types that I would recommend for this flavor, with bing cherries being my first choice. Leave the cherries out for a few days on your kitchen counter to get them extra ripe and juicy for the gelato. Removing the pit from each cherry requires a little more work, but the end result is a nicely flavored gelato with flecks of cherry throughout.

Like other gelato artisans, I've chosen to make Ciliegia into a dairy-based flavor as opposed to a sorbet. I love the combination of cherries and cream, and I think the fruit is best represented this way.

Ingredients

2 ounces / 56 grams milk powder

7.05 ounces / 200 grams
    granulated sugar

1 pinch kosher salt

0.7 ounce / 20 grams tapioca starch

6.75 ounces / 192 grams heavy cream

24.15 ounces / 685 grams whole milk

1.27 ounces / 36 grams light corn syrup

5.65 ounces / 160 grams fresh cherries, stems
    removed, pitted, and finely chopped
    (about 32 cherries)

Yield: About 1.5 quarts / 1.42 liters

Prepare

1. Mix the milk powder, sugar, salt, and tapioca starch in a bowl.

2. Add the heavy cream and whole milk and whisk well to incorporate all of the dry ingredients into the liquid.

3. Whisk in the corn syrup.

Cook

4. Pour the mixture into a 2.5-quart / 2.36-liter saucepan, using a spatula to scrape the sides of the bowl. Place the saucepan on medium-high heat and cook, whisking continuously to prevent any burning or clumping. Whisk slowly in the beginning and increase speed as the mixture gets warmer and begins to steam and thicken. It should thicken without boiling after 8 to 12 minutes on the heat; watch carefully so it doesn't burn. Once the mixture has thickened enough to coat the back of a spoon, continue cooking 15 seconds longer, whisking vigorously. Then immediately remove from the heat.

How to Tell If Gelato Is Done

- *The gelato thickens into a firm but easy-to-remove mass and pulls away from the sides of the canister as it is being churned*

- *Some of the gelato is frozen to the canister sides, and the machine paddle is moving more slowly through the gelato*

- *The gelato has been churning for at least 30 minutes*

Cherries

Cherry gelato in Italy is often called amarena *because of the popular use of amarena cherries in gelato production. These cherries, found in the Emilia-Romagna region of Italy, are small, dark in color, and more bitter than the cherries we are used to in America. Although one can find amarena cherries packaged in syrup by the famous Italian producer Fabbri, I've chosen to use fresh cherries for this recipe.*

Freeze

5. Pour the mixture into a clean glass or stainless-steel bowl. Whisk in the cherries and any juice.

6. Lay plastic wrap directly on the surface to prevent a skin from forming on top. Allow the mixture to cool 30 to 45 minutes, until no longer hot. Then place it in the refrigerator to cool completely, about 4 hours. If the mixture needs to be used right away, submerge most of the bowl in an ice bath and let it sit 30 to 40 minutes, refreshing the ice as necessary.

7. Once the mixture has cooled completely and thickened further, pour it into the bowl of the gelato machine and churn the gelato according to the manufacturer's directions. The gelato will expand and should spin until it's thick and creamy but still soft enough to scoop into a storage container, about 30 to 55 minutes.

8. Using a rubber spatula, scoop the gelato into a storage container.

9. Press a piece of plastic wrap or parchment paper directly on the surface of the gelato, seal the container with an airtight lid, and put it in the freezer.

10. Freeze at least 4 to 5 hours. When ready, the gelato should be firm enough to scoop but soft and creamy in texture.

Serve

11. Enjoy the fresh gelato as soon as possible. If using after 1 day, allow 8 to 12 minutes for the gelato to soften outside of the freezer before eating.

CREMA DI AGRUMI
Citrus Cream

A traditional Sicilian flavor, Crema di Agrumi is close in taste to an American Creamsicle. The original version calls for an array of citrus because Sicily is known for its many high-quality varieties, but I've kept this recipe simple yet bold with lemon, orange, and a little lime zest. If you enjoy a strong citrus flavor and are looking for a little texture, finely chop a few strips of lemon and orange rind and add to the base before cooking.

Ingredients

2 ounces / 56 grams milk powder

7.05 ounces / 200 grams granulated sugar

0.7 ounce / 20 grams tapioca starch

6.75 ounces / 192 grams heavy cream

24.15 ounces / 685 grams whole milk

1.15 ounces / 33 grams light corn syrup

0.35 ounce / 10 grams strained, fresh-squeezed lemon juice (just over 2 teaspoons)

0.35 ounce / 10 grams strained, fresh-squeezed orange juice (just over 2 teaspoons)

Zest of 3 lemons, 2 oranges, and 1 lime, preferably organic, finely chopped

Yield: About 1.5 quarts / 1.42 liters

Prepare

1. Mix the milk powder, sugar, and tapioca starch in a bowl.

2. Add the heavy cream and whole milk and whisk well to incorporate all of the dry ingredients into the liquid.

3. Whisk in the corn syrup, lemon and orange juices, and all of the zest.

Cook

4. Pour the mixture into a 2.5-quart / 2.36-liter saucepan, using a spatula to scrape the sides of the bowl. Place the saucepan on medium-high heat and cook, whisking continuously to prevent any burning or clumping. Whisk slowly in the beginning and increase speed as the mixture gets warmer and begins to steam and thicken. It should thicken without boiling after 8 to 12 minutes on the heat; watch carefully so it doesn't burn. Once the mixture has thickened enough to coat the back of a spoon, continue cooking 15 seconds longer, whisking vigorously. Then immediately remove from the heat.

Freeze

5. Pour the mixture into a clean glass or stainless-steel bowl and lay plastic wrap directly on the surface to prevent a skin from forming on top. Allow the mixture to sit 30 to 45 minutes, until no longer hot. Then place it in the refrigerator to cool completely, about 4 hours. If the mixture needs to be used right away, submerge most of the bowl in an ice bath and let it sit 30 to 40 minutes, refreshing the ice as necessary.

6. Once the mixture has cooled completely and thickened further, pour it into the bowl of the gelato machine and churn the gelato according to the manufacturer's directions. The gelato will expand and should spin until it's thick and creamy but still soft enough to scoop into a storage container, about 30 to 55 minutes.

7. Using a rubber spatula, scoop the gelato into a storage container.

8. Press a piece of plastic wrap or parchment paper directly on the surface of the gelato, seal the container with an airtight lid, and put it in the freezer.

9. Freeze at least 4 to 5 hours. When ready, the gelato should be firm enough to scoop but soft and creamy in texture.

Serve

10. Enjoy the fresh gelato as soon as possible. If using after 1 day, allow 7 to 10 minutes for the gelato to soften outside of the freezer before eating.

CANNELLA
Cinnamon

This Cannella gelato is bold and sweet. It is one of my favorite flavors and, until recently, was not commonly available in America. I've incorporated an egg yolk into the recipe to help round out the texture provided by the ground cinnamon, but it also helps to give the gelato more body.

Cinnamon gelato is a dream come true for any cinnamon and sugar lover, and it's perfect served on warm apple crisp during a cool fall day.

Ingredients

2 ounces / 56 grams milk powder

7.6 ounces / 215 grams granulated sugar

0.2 ounce / 6 grams ground cinnamon

0.7 ounce / 20 grams tapioca starch

6.75 ounces / 192 grams heavy cream

24.15 ounces / 685 grams whole milk

1.15 ounces / 33 grams light corn syrup

1 egg yolk

Yield: About 1.5 quarts / 1.42 liters

Prepare

1. Mix the milk powder, sugar, cinnamon, and tapioca starch in a bowl.
2. Add the heavy cream and whole milk and whisk well to incorporate all of the dry ingredients into the liquid.
3. Whisk in the corn syrup and egg yolk.

Cook

4. Pour the mixture into a 2.5-quart / 2.36-liter saucepan, using a spatula to scrape the sides of the bowl. Place the saucepan on medium-high heat and cook, whisking continuously to prevent any burning or clumping. Whisk slowly in the beginning and increase speed as the mixture gets warmer and begins to steam and thicken. It should thicken without boiling after 8 to 12 minutes on the heat; watch carefully so it doesn't burn. Once the mixture has thickened enough to coat the back of a spoon, continue cooking 15 seconds longer, whisking vigorously. Then immediately remove from the heat.

Freeze

5. Pour the mixture into a clean glass or stainless-steel bowl and lay plastic wrap directly on the surface to prevent a skin from forming on top. Allow the mixture to sit 30 to 45 minutes, until no longer hot. Then place it in the refrigerator to cool completely, about 4 hours. If the mixture needs to be used right away, submerge most of the bowl in an ice bath and let it sit 30 to 40 minutes, refreshing the ice as necessary.
6. Once the mixture has cooled completely and thickened further, pour it into the bowl of the gelato machine and churn the gelato according to the manufacturer's directions. The gelato will expand and should spin until it's thick and creamy but still soft enough to scoop into a storage container, about 30 to 55 minutes.
7. Using a rubber spatula, scoop the gelato into a storage container.
8. Press a piece of plastic wrap or parchment paper directly on the surface of the gelato, seal the container with an airtight lid, and put it in the freezer.
9. Freeze at least 4 to 5 hours. When ready, the gelato should be firm enough to scoop but soft and creamy in texture.

Serve

10. Enjoy the fresh gelato as soon as possible. If using after 1 day, allow 8 to 10 minutes for the gelato to soften outside of the freezer before eating.

CREMA DI COCCO
Coconut Cream

Crema di Cocco gelato gets its taste and texture from strongly flavored coconut flakes. I recommend using the sweetened variety for this recipe, but unsweetened will work. The vanilla extract gives this flavor a familiar taste as coconut and vanilla are often paired together. Use a high-quality vanilla extract, such as a brand of Madagascar vanilla, which should be available in the baking aisle of most supermarkets.

Coconut Cream is classically paired with chocolate. It's like eating a frozen Mounds bar!

Ingredients

2 ounces / 56 grams milk powder

7.05 ounces / 200 grams granulated sugar

1 pinch kosher salt

0.7 ounce / 20 grams tapioca starch

6.75 ounces / 192 grams heavy cream

24.15 ounces / 685 grams whole milk

1.15 ounces / 33 grams light corn syrup

0.15 ounce / 4 grams vanilla extract

4.1 ounces / 115 grams sweetened coconut flakes

Yield: About 1.5 quarts / 1.42 liters

Prepare

1. Mix the milk powder, sugar, salt, and tapioca starch in a bowl.

2. Add the heavy cream and whole milk and whisk well to incorporate all of the dry ingredients into the liquid.

3. Add the corn syrup, vanilla extract, and coconut flakes. Blend with an immersion blender so that the coconut flakes are reduced to small pieces and fully incorporated into the base.

Cook

4. Pour the mixture into a 2.5-quart / 2.36-liter saucepan, using a spatula to scrape the sides of the bowl. Place the saucepan on medium-high heat and cook, whisking continuously to prevent any burning or clumping. Whisk slowly in the beginning and increase speed as the mixture gets warmer and begins to steam and thicken. It should thicken without boiling after 8 to 12 minutes on the heat; watch carefully so it doesn't burn. Once the mixture has thickened enough to coat the back of a spoon, continue cooking 15 seconds longer, whisking vigorously. Then immediately remove from the heat.

Freeze

5. Pour the mixture into a clean glass or stainless-steel bowl and lay plastic wrap directly on the surface to prevent a skin from forming on top. Allow the mixture to sit 30 to 45 minutes, until no longer hot. Then place it in the refrigerator to cool about 4 hours. If the mixture needs to be used right away, submerge most of the bowl in an ice bath and let it sit 30 to 40 minutes, refreshing the ice as necessary.

6. Once the mixture has cooled completely and thickened further, pour it into the bowl of the gelato machine and churn the gelato according to the manufacturer's directions. The gelato will expand and should spin until it's thick and creamy but still soft enough to scoop into a storage container, about 30 to 55 minutes.

7. Using a rubber spatula, scoop the gelato into a storage container.

8. Press a piece of plastic wrap or parchment paper directly on the surface of the gelato, seal the container with an airtight lid, and put it in the freezer.

9. Freeze at least 4 to 5 hours. When ready, the gelato should be firm enough to scoop but soft and creamy in texture.

Serve

10. Enjoy the fresh gelato as soon as possible. If using after 1 day, allow 7 to 10 minutes for the gelato to soften outside of the freezer before eating.

AMARETTO
Italian Almond Cookie

Made with one of my favorite kinds of Italian cookie, Amaretto gelato is sweet and has a strong almond flavor. I use the classic Lazzaroni cookies for this recipe, but any type of store-bought amaretto cookie, including Lazzaroni Amaretti Cookie Snaps, will work. Amaretto is a fun Italian-themed flavor that can be paired with a simple cake or fruit crostata ("tart").

Ingredients

1.6 ounces / 46 grams milk powder

6.35 ounces / 180 grams granulated sugar

0.7 ounce / 20 grams tapioca starch

6.75 ounces / 192 grams heavy cream

24.15 ounces / 685 grams whole milk

0.95 ounce / 27 grams light corn syrup

0.2 ounce / 5 grams almond extract or amaretto liqueur

2.1 ounces / 60 grams *amaretti* ("almond cookies"), crushed by hand or chopped, plus extra for garnish

Yield: About 1.5 quarts / 1.42 liters

Prepare

1. Mix the milk powder, sugar, and tapioca starch in a bowl.

2. Add the heavy cream and whole milk and whisk well to incorporate all of the dry ingredients into the liquid.

3. Add the corn syrup, the almond extract or liqueur, and amaretti. Blend with an immersion blender to fully incorporate these ingredients, making sure no large pieces of the amaretti remain.

Cook

4. Pour the mixture into a 2.5-quart / 2.36-liter saucepan, using a spatula to scrape the sides of the bowl. Place the saucepan on medium-high heat and cook, whisking continuously to prevent any burning or clumping. Whisk slowly in the beginning and increase speed as the mixture gets warmer and begins to steam and thicken. It should thicken without boiling after 8 to 12 minutes on the heat; watch carefully so it doesn't burn. Once the mixture has thickened enough to coat the back of a spoon, continue cooking 15 seconds longer, whisking vigorously. Then immediately remove from the heat.

Freeze

5. Pour the mixture into a clean glass or stainless-steel bowl and lay plastic wrap directly on the surface to prevent a skin from forming on top. Allow the mixture to sit 30 to 45 minutes, until no longer hot. Then place it in the refrigerator to cool completely, about 4 hours. If the mixture needs to be used right away, submerge most of the bowl in an ice bath and let it sit 30 to 40 minutes, refreshing the ice as necessary.

6. Once the mixture has cooled completely and thickened further, pour it into the bowl of the gelato machine and churn the gelato according to the manufacturer's directions. The gelato will expand and should spin until it's thick and creamy but still soft enough to scoop into a storage container, about 30 to 55 minutes.

7. Using a rubber spatula, scoop the gelato into a storage container.

8. Press a piece of plastic wrap or parchment paper directly on the surface of the gelato, seal the container with an airtight lid, and put it in the freezer.

9. Freeze at least 4 to 5 hours. When ready, the gelato should be firm enough to scoop but soft and creamy in texture.

Serve

10. Enjoy the fresh gelato as soon as possible. If using after 1 day, allow 7 to 10 minutes for the gelato to soften outside of the freezer before eating. Sprinkle crushed amaretti cookies on top.

CARAMELLO
Caramel

At Morano Gelato, we're fortunate to have a special caramel sauce made for our gelato by Red Kite Candy of Thetford, Vermont—a company that makes the best caramel I have ever had. If you're up for a challenge with potentially excellent results, purchase their caramels online at redkitecandy.com and make a sauce out of them (see recipe page 71).

You can, of course, use your own caramel sauce or a commercially prepared one that you love for this recipe. I used Wicked Good Caramel Topping by Schlotterbeck & Foss. This caramel appeals to me both for the fact that it is produced in the neighboring state of Maine and for its intensely delicious flavor. Remember, the stronger the flavor of the caramel and the purer the ingredients, the better tasting your gelato will be. Just make sure that the sauce you choose is fluid enough to dissolve into the gelato base without leaving any hard caramel lumps.

I've made this Caramello gelato recipe with only a slight salty finish. Those looking for a saltier version can add an additional 3 pinches of salt to the recipe or garnish the gelato with sea salt flakes.

Ingredients

2 ounces / 56 grams milk powder

6 ounces / 170 grams granulated sugar

1 pinch kosher salt

0.7 ounce / 20 grams tapioca starch

7.4 ounces / 210 grams heavy cream

24.15 ounces / 685 grams whole milk

1 ounce / 28 grams light corn syrup

3.5 ounces / 100 grams caramel sauce, plus a
little extra to drizzle on top (optional)

1 egg yolk

Yield: About 1.5 quarts / 1.42 liters

Prepare

1. Mix the milk powder, sugar, salt, and tapioca starch in a bowl.

2. Add the heavy cream and whole milk and whisk well to incorporate all of the dry ingredients into the liquid.

3. Whisk in the corn syrup, caramel sauce, and egg yolk.

Cook

4. Pour the mixture into a 2.5-quart / 2.36-liter saucepan, using a spatula to scrape the sides of the bowl. Place the saucepan on medium-high heat and cook, whisking continuously to prevent any burning or clumping. Whisk slowly in the beginning and increase speed as the mixture gets warmer and begins to steam and thicken. It should thicken without boiling after 8 to 12 minutes on the heat; watch carefully so it doesn't burn. Once the mixture has thickened enough to coat the back of a spoon, continue cooking 15 seconds longer, whisking vigorously. Then immediately remove from the heat.

Why We Love Salty and Sweet

What make this taste combination so desirable? One theory is that our body needs salt but doesn't store it, so we have a built in craving for it. Sugar means calories and energy— something else our body wants. Two simultaneous positive biological responses make for one pleasurable taste sensation that's simply irresistible.

Freeze

5. Pour the mixture into a clean glass or stainless-steel bowl and lay plastic wrap directly on the surface to prevent a skin from forming on top. Allow the mixture to sit 30 to 45 minutes, until no longer hot. Then place it in the refrigerator to cool completely, about 4 hours. If the mixture needs to be used right away, submerge most of the bowl in an ice bath and let it sit 30 to 40 minutes, refreshing the ice as necessary.

6. Once the mixture has cooled completely and thickened further, pour it into the bowl of the gelato machine and churn the gelato according to the manufacturer's directions. The gelato will expand and should spin until it's thick and creamy but still soft enough to scoop into a storage container, about 30 to 55 minutes. Because of its high sugar content, Carmel gelato will be slightly softer than other flavors when ready.

7. Using a rubber spatula, scoop the gelato into a storage container.

8. Press a piece of plastic wrap or parchment paper directly on the surface of the gelato, seal the container with an airtight lid, and put it in the freezer.

9. Freeze at least 4 to 5 hours. When ready, the gelato should be firm enough to scoop but soft and creamy in texture.

Serve

10. Enjoy the fresh gelato as soon as possible. If using after 1 day, allow 5 to 8 minutes for the gelato to soften outside of the freezer before eating. Drizzle a little caramel sauce on top, if desired.

Caramel Sauce
(from Red Kite caramels)

3 tablespoons milk or cream
1 package (4 ounces / 113 grams) of your favorite Red Kite caramel flavor

Add the milk or cream to the caramels and slowly heat on the stove top, stirring constantly. Heat only until the caramels have melted and the milk or cream has been incorporated. If using a microwave, heat the caramels and milk or cream on low power, stopping to stir a couple of times during the melting process.

CASSATA
Sicilian Cake with Candied Fruit

When asked about my favorite gelato flavors, Cassata is second only to dark chocolate. Cassata is a well-known Sicilian cake consisting of candied fruit, ricotta, citrus, almond, and chocolate, layered on top of a liqueur-soaked sponge cake. The cake is finished with a layer of marzipan and brightly colored icing, and garnished with large pieces of candied fruit. This gelato contains all the same flavors, only in frozen form.

Ingredients

2 ounces / 56 grams milk powder

7.05 ounces / 200 grams granulated sugar

1 pinch kosher salt

0.7 ounce / 20 grams tapioca starch

7.05 ounces / 200 grams heavy cream

21.15 ounces / 600 grams whole milk

1.15 ounces / 33 grams light corn syrup

3.55 ounces / 100 grams whole cow's-milk ricotta

0.2 ounce / 5 grams almond extract

Zest of 1 lemon and 1 orange

1.75 ounces / 50 grams 60% to 70% dark chocolate, finely chopped

2.1 ounces / 60 grams candied fruit or maraschino cherries, finely chopped

Yield: About 1.5 quarts / 1.42 liters

Prepare

1. Mix the milk powder, sugar, salt, and tapioca starch in a bowl.

2. Add the heavy cream and whole milk and whisk well to incorporate all of the dry ingredients into the liquid.

3. Whisk in the corn syrup, ricotta, almond extract, and lemon and orange zest.

Cook

4. Pour the mixture into a 2.5-quart / 2.36-liter saucepan, using a spatula to scrape the sides of the bowl. Place the saucepan on medium-high heat and cook, whisking continuously to prevent any burning or clumping. Whisk slowly in the beginning and increase speed as the mixture gets warmer and begins to steam and thicken. It should thicken without boiling after 8 to 12 minutes on the heat; watch carefully so it doesn't burn. Once the mixture has thickened enough to coat the back of a spoon, continue cooking 15 seconds longer, whisking vigorously. Then immediately remove from the heat.

Freeze

5. Pour the mixture into a clean glass or stainless-steel bowl and lay plastic wrap directly on the surface to prevent a skin from forming on top. Allow the mixture to sit 30 to 45 minutes, until no longer hot. Then place in the refrigerator to cool completely, about 4 hours. If the mixture needs to be used right away, submerge most of the bowl in an ice bath and let it sit 30 to 40 minutes, refreshing the ice as necessary.

6. Once the mixture has cooled completely and thickened further, pour it into the bowl of the gelato machine and gently stir in the chocolate and candied fruit or maraschino cherries. Churn the gelato according to the manufacturer's directions. The gelato will expand and should spin until it's thick and creamy but still soft enough to scoop into a storage container, about 30 to 55 minutes.

7. Using a rubber spatula, scoop the gelato into a storage container.

8. Press a piece of plastic wrap or parchment paper directly on the surface of the gelato, seal the container with an airtight lid, and put it in the freezer.

9. Freeze at least 4 to 5 hours. When ready, the gelato should be firm enough to scoop but soft and creamy in texture.

Serve

10. Enjoy the fresh gelato as soon as possible. If using after 1 day, allow 7 to 10 minutes for the gelato to soften outside of the freezer before eating.

BACIO
Chocolate-Hazelnut Kiss

Baci ("kisses") candies, chocolates filled with hazelnuts, are the inspiration for this gelato flavor. These signature Italian chocolates, wrapped in silver foil with blue stars, have love quotes tucked inside and are now available in many American shops.

Ingredients

1.25 ounces / 35 grams milk powder

7.05 ounces / 200 grams granulated sugar

2 pinches kosher salt

1.05 ounces / 30 grams cacao powder

0.7 ounce / 20 grams tapioca starch

6.75 ounces / 192 grams heavy cream

24.15 ounces / 685 grams whole milk

1.15 ounces / 33 grams light corn syrup

2.1 ounces / 60 grams whole hazelnuts, roasted and chopped

1 egg yolk

Yield: About 1.5 quarts / 1.42 liters

Prepare

1. Mix the milk powder, sugar, salt, cacao powder, and tapioca starch in a bowl.

2. Add the heavy cream and whole milk and whisk well to incorporate all of the dry ingredients into the liquid.

3. Add the corn syrup and hazelnuts. Blend with an immersion blender so that the hazelnuts are reduced to smaller pieces and are incorporated into the base.

4. Whisk in the egg yolk.

Cook

5. Pour the mixture into a 2.5-quart / 2.36-liter saucepan, using a spatula to scrape the sides of the bowl. Place the saucepan on medium-high heat and cook, whisking continuously to prevent any burning or clumping. Whisk slowly in the beginning and increase speed as the mixture gets warmer and begins to steam and thicken. It should thicken without boiling after 8 to 12 minutes on the heat; watch carefully so it doesn't burn. Once the mixture has thickened enough to coat the back of a spoon, continue cooking 15 seconds longer, whisking vigorously. Then immediately remove from the heat.

Freeze

6. Pour the mixture into a clean glass or stainless-steel bowl and lay plastic wrap directly on the surface to prevent a skin from forming on top. Allow the mixture to sit 30 to 45 minutes, until no longer hot. Then place in the refrigerator to cool completely, about 4 hours. If the mixture needs to be used right away, submerge most of the bowl in an ice bath and let it sit 30 to 40 minutes, refreshing the ice as necessary.

7. Once the mixture has cooled completely and thickened further, pour it into the bowl of the gelato machine and churn the gelato according to the manufacturer's directions. The gelato will expand and should spin until it's thick and creamy but still soft enough to scoop into a storage container, about 30 to 55 minutes.

8. Using a rubber spatula, scoop the gelato into a storage container.

9. Press a piece of plastic wrap or parchment paper directly on the surface of the gelato, seal the container with an airtight lid, and put it in the freezer.

10. Freeze at least 4 to 5 hours. When ready, the gelato should be firm enough to scoop but soft and creamy in texture.

Serve

11. Enjoy the fresh gelato as soon as possible. If using after 1 day, allow 7 to 10 minutes for the gelato to soften outside of the freezer before eating.

CIOCCOLATO E PEPERONCINO
Chocolate and Red Chili Pepper

The Cioccolato e Peperoncino flavor delivers a chilled temperature with a hot kick at the finish. It is tantalizing to those who love spicy foods or enjoy opposing sensations, such as hot and cold, at once. This recipe includes cinnamon, which is commonly paired with chocolate and red chili pepper. I use cayenne pepper instead of red pepper flakes so that the texture of the chocolate remains smooth, but I garnish the finished gelato with red pepper flakes.

Lastly, I use a dark-chocolate gelato base for this recipe to give a rich depth of flavor and a palate-pleasing backdrop for the spice.

However you make Cioccalato e Peperoncino gelato, it is sure to offer a deliciously unexpected taste surprise.

Ingredients

1.25 ounces / 35 grams milk powder

7.95 ounces / 225 grams granulated sugar

2 pinches kosher salt

1.05 ounces / 30 grams cacao powder

2 pinches ground cayenne pepper

3 pinches ground cinnamon

0.7 ounce / 20 grams tapioca starch

6.75 ounces / 192 grams heavy cream

24.15 ounces / 685 grams whole milk

1.4 ounces / 40 grams light corn syrup

2 egg yolks

0.9 ounce / 25 grams 100% dark chocolate, finely chopped

1.4 ounces / 40 grams 60% to 70% dark chocolate, finely chopped

Red pepper flakes for garnish (optional)

Yield: About 1.5 quarts / 1.42 liters

Prepare

1. Mix the milk powder, sugar, salt, cacao powder, cayenne pepper, cinnamon, and tapioca starch in a bowl.
2. Add the heavy cream and whole milk and whisk well to incorporate all of the dry ingredients into the liquid.
3. Whisk in the corn syrup and egg yolks.
4. Put both kinds of dark chocolate into a separate glass or heatproof bowl that's large enough to hold the entire base once it has finished cooking. Set aside and begin cooking the base.

Cook

5. Pour the mixture for the base into a 2.5-quart / 2.36-liter saucepan, using a spatula to scrape the sides of the bowl. Place the saucepan on medium-high heat and cook, whisking continuously to prevent any burning or clumping. Whisk slowly in the beginning and increase speed as the mixture gets warmer and begins to steam and thicken. It should thicken without boiling after 8 to 12 minutes on the heat; watch carefully so it doesn't burn. Once the mixture has thickened enough to coat the back of a spoon, continue cooking 15 seconds longer, whisking vigorously. Then immediately remove from the heat.

Freeze

6. Pour half of the hot base into the bowl containing the chocolate and whisk to melt the chocolate and incorporate it into the mixture. Finish by carefully whisking in the rest of the hot base, making sure all of the chocolate is fully melted and mixed in.

7. Lay plastic wrap directly on the surface to prevent a skin from forming on top. Allow the mixture to sit 30 to 45 minutes, until no longer hot. Then place in the refrigerator to cool completely, about 4 hours. If the mixture needs to be used right away, submerge most of the bowl in an ice bath and let it sit 30 to 40 minutes, refreshing the ice as necessary.

8. Once the mixture has cooled completely and thickened further, pour it into the bowl of the gelato machine and churn the gelato according to the manufacturer's directions. The gelato will expand and should spin until it's thick and creamy but still soft enough to scoop into a storage container, about 30 to 55 minutes.

9. Using a rubber spatula, scoop the gelato into a storage container.

10. Press a piece of plastic wrap or parchment paper directly on the surface of the gelato, seal the container with an airtight lid, and put it in the freezer.

11. Freeze at least 4 to 5 hours. When ready, the gelato should be firm enough to scoop but soft and creamy in texture.

Serve

12. Enjoy the fresh gelato as soon as possible. If using after 1 day, allow 10 to 15 minutes for the gelato to soften outside of the freezer before eating. Garnish with red pepper flakes, if desired.

Cayenne

Cayenne pepper is potent, so the recipe only calls for a small amount, but if you like more heat, you can use more. You can also choose a different kind of pepper (in powder form) if cayenne is not to your liking. Just remember that the gelato will take on the flavor of whatever pepper you use. If you choose to adjust the recipe, I recommend tasting the base before cooking it to ensure proper proportions.

GELSOMINO
Jasmine

The first time I tasted Gelsomino in Italy ten years ago, I was so surprised that a gelato flavor like this existed. It was sweet and milky with a flowery finish. Nowadays, unusual flavors are becoming more common, and flower extracts and essences are more readily available. I created this recipe using a jasmine essence by Dragonfly, a company I found online. I recommend searching online or in a local Asian specialty food store for a high-quality jasmine essence or extract. Make sure that it can be used in cooking and isn't an oil.

Jasmine gelato is perfect on a spring or summer day with fresh berries, or by itself to surprise and delight guests with its unique flavor.

Ingredients

2 ounces / 56 grams milk powder

6.35 ounces / 180 grams granulated sugar

0.7 ounce / 20 grams tapioca starch

7.4 ounces / 210 grams heavy cream

24.15 ounces / 685 grams whole milk

1 ounce / 28 grams light corn syrup

0.4 ounce / 12 grams jasmine essence
or extract

Yield: About 1.5 quarts / 1.42 liters

Prepare

1. Mix the milk powder, sugar, and tapioca starch in a bowl.
2. Add the heavy cream and whole milk and whisk well to incorporate all of the dry ingredients into the liquid.
3. Whisk in the corn syrup and jasmine essence or extract.

Cook

4. Pour the mixture into a 2.5-quart / 2.36-liter saucepan, using a spatula to scrape the sides of the bowl. Place the saucepan on medium-high heat and cook, whisking continuously to prevent any burning or clumping. Whisk slowly in the beginning and increase speed as the mixture gets warmer and begins to steam and thicken. It should thicken without boiling after 8 to 12 minutes on the heat; watch carefully so it doesn't burn. Once the mixture has thickened enough to coat the back of a spoon, continue cooking 15 seconds longer, whisking vigorously. Then immediately remove from the heat.

Freeze

5. Pour the mixture into a clean glass or stainless-steel bowl and lay plastic wrap directly on the surface to prevent a skin from forming on top. Allow the mixture to sit 30 to 45 minutes, until no longer hot. Then place in the refrigerator to cool completely, about 4 hours. If the mixture needs to be used right away, submerge most of the bowl in an ice bath and let it sit 30 to 40 minutes, refreshing the ice as necessary.

Jasmine

Originally from Asia, jasmine is mentioned in Chinese writings as far back as the ninth century. Its famous aroma comes from an oil in the petals, and that is the part of the plant where the flavoring originates.

Most jasmine extracts or essences, if produced correctly, should be strong in flavor, and a little will go a long way.

6. Once the mixture has cooled completely and thickened further, pour it into the bowl of the gelato machine and churn the gelato according to the manufacturer's directions. The gelato will expand and should spin until it's thick and creamy but still soft enough to scoop into a storage container, about 30 to 55 minutes.

7. Using a rubber spatula, scoop the gelato into a storage container.

8. Press a piece of plastic wrap or parchment paper directly on the surface of the gelato, seal the container with an airtight lid, and put it in the freezer.

9. Freeze at least 4 to 5 hours. When ready, the gelato should be firm enough to scoop but soft and creamy in texture.

Serve

10. Enjoy the fresh gelato as soon as possible. If using after 1 day, allow 7 to 10 minutes for the gelato to soften outside of the freezer before eating.

ZUPPA INGLESE
English Pudding

Zuppa Inglese, literally translated as "English soup," is a unique flavor inspired by the English trifle but with an Italian twist. The base of this gelato is custard with a little nutmeg and rum. Once frozen, the gelato is layered with pieces of sponge cake soaked in a bright red Florentine liqueur called alchermes. This liqueur may be hard to find so, if necessary, you can substitute grenadine and rum. Either homemade or store-bought sponge cake will work here. A pastry brush should be used to spread the liqueur on the cake for the assembly of this gelato trifle. For an easy alternative if you don't wish to put together a trifle, serve the gelato with sponge cake.

The flavor of Zuppa Inglese evokes memories of Christmas pudding, making it a wonderful choice for the holidays or other festive occasions.

Ingredients

1.6 ounces / 46 grams milk powder

7.6 ounces / 215 grams granulated sugar

1 pinch kosher salt

1 pinch ground nutmeg

0.7 ounce / 20 grams tapioca starch

8.8 ounces / 250 grams heavy cream

21.15 ounces / 600 grams whole milk

0.4 ounce / 12 grams dark rum

1.15 ounces / 33 grams light corn syrup

4 egg yolks

6.55 ounces / 185 grams alchermes*

6.55 ounces / 185 grams powdered sugar

13.1 ounces / 370 grams warm water

Sponge cake, for layering

* If you cannot find alchermes, you may substitute equal parts of grenadine and rum in place of the alchermes, powdered sugar, and water mixture.

Yield: About 1.5 quarts / 1.42 liters

Prepare

1. Mix the milk powder, sugar, salt, nutmeg, and tapioca starch in a bowl.
2. Add the heavy cream, whole milk, and rum and whisk well to incorporate all of the dry ingredients into the liquid.
3. Whisk in the corn syrup and egg yolks.

Cook

4. Pour the mixture into a 2.5-quart / 2.36-liter saucepan, using a spatula to scrape the sides of the bowl. Place the saucepan on medium-high heat and cook, whisking continuously to prevent any burning or clumping. Whisk slowly in the beginning and increase speed as the mixture gets warmer and begins to steam and thicken. It should thicken without boiling after 8 to 12 minutes on the heat; watch carefully so it doesn't burn. Once the mixture has thickened enough to coat the back of a spoon, continue cooking 15 seconds longer, whisking vigorously. Then immediately remove from the heat.

Freeze

5. Pour the mixture into a clean glass or stainless-steel bowl and lay plastic wrap directly on the surface to prevent a skin from forming on top. Allow the mixture to sit 30 to 45 minutes, until no longer hot. Then place in the refrigerator to cool completely, about 4 hours. If the mixture needs to be used right away, submerge most of the bowl in an ice bath and let it sit 30 to 40 minutes, refreshing the ice as necessary.

6. Once the mixture has cooled completely and thickened further, pour it into the bowl of the gelato machine and churn the gelato according to the manufacturer's directions. The gelato will expand and should spin until it's thick and creamy but still soft enough to scoop into a storage container, about 30 to 55 minutes. This gelato will be slightly softer than other flavors due to the alcohol content.

7. Using a rubber spatula, scoop the gelato into a storage container.

8. Press a piece of plastic wrap or parchment paper directly on the surface of the gelato, seal the container with an airtight lid, and put it in the freezer.

9. Freeze at least 4 hours, until semi-firm.

10. While the gelato is in the freezer, prepare the sponge cake and liqueur for the trifle. Mix alchermes, powdered sugar, and water in a small bowl. (If using grenadine and rum, combine equal parts of both.) Whisk well.

11. Cut the sponge cake into thin slices and fit a single layer of them into the bottom of a small trifle bowl or other quart-sized glass dish. Brush the liqueur mixture onto each piece of sponge cake.

12. Remove the gelato from the freezer and, working quickly to avoid the gelato melting, spread it on top of the cake. Repeat layers of liqueur-soaked cake and gelato until the dish is full. The gelato layers should be bigger than the cake layers, and I recommend no more than three layers of cake total. (If the gelato begins to melt, you can put the trifle and gelato in the freezer to firm up before finishing.) The trifle can be finished with either a layer of gelato or cake on top. If finishing with gelato, you can crumble pieces of cake over the gelato for garnish when serving.

13. Cover the gelato trifle with a lid or plastic wrap and freeze for another 2 to 4 hours, or until the gelato is firm enough to scoop but still soft and creamy in texture.

Serve

14. Enjoy the fresh gelato trifle within 24 hours.

MALAGA
Marsala Raisin

Although I've never been a big fan of raisins, I love this gelato flavor. Italy's Malaga is comparable to our rum raisin, but the Marsala wine gives this gelato an unfamiliar but appealing complexity. It's sweet, easy to make, and easy to eat. Just as with Crema all'Uovo (page 34), I find that a sweet Marsala wine is best for this recipe, but any Marsala wine will work.

Ingredients

2 ounces / 56 grams milk powder

6.35 ounces / 180 grams granulated sugar

0.7 ounce / 20 grams tapioca starch

6.75 ounces / 192 grams heavy cream

24.15 ounces / 685 grams whole milk

1.15 ounces / 33 grams light corn syrup

2.65 ounces / 75 grams raisins, finely chopped

0.7 ounce / 20 grams sweet Marsala wine

Yield: About 1.5 quarts / 1.42 liters

Prepare

1. Mix the milk powder, sugar, and tapioca starch in a bowl.
2. Add the heavy cream and whole milk and whisk well to incorporate all of the dry ingredients into the liquid.
3. Whisk in the corn syrup, raisins, and Marsala wine.

Cook

4. Pour the mixture into a 2.5-quart / 2.36-liter saucepan, using a spatula to scrape the sides of the bowl. Place the saucepan on medium-high heat and cook, whisking continuously to prevent any burning or clumping. Whisk slowly in the beginning and increase speed as the mixture gets warmer and begins to steam and thicken. It should thicken without boiling after 8 to 12 minutes on the heat; watch carefully so it doesn't burn. Once the mixture has thickened enough to coat the back of a spoon, continue cooking 15 seconds longer, whisking vigorously. Then immediately remove from the heat.

Freeze

5. Pour the mixture into a clean glass or stainless-steel bowl and lay plastic wrap directly on the surface to prevent a skin from forming on top. Allow the mixture to sit 30 to 45 minutes, until no longer hot. Then place in the refrigerator to cool completely, about 4 hours. If the mixture needs to be used right away, submerge most of the bowl in an ice bath and let it sit 30 to 40 minutes, refreshing the ice as necessary.
6. Once the mixture has cooled completely and thickened further, pour it into the bowl of the gelato machine and churn the gelato according to the manufacturer's directions. The gelato will expand and should spin until it's thick and creamy but still soft enough to scoop into a storage container, about 30 to 55 minutes.
7. Using a rubber spatula, scoop the gelato into a storage container.
8. Press a piece of plastic wrap or parchment paper directly on the surface of the gelato, seal the container with an airtight lid, and put it in the freezer.
9. Freeze at least 4 to 5 hours. When ready, the gelato should be firm enough to scoop but soft and creamy in texture.

Serve

10. Enjoy the fresh gelato as soon as possible. If using after 1 day, allow 7 to 10 minutes for the gelato to soften outside of the freezer before eating.

MENTA
Mint

Mint is a great flavor to enjoy all year round, with variations possible to suit the season or your imagination (such as adding pieces of finely chopped chocolate or crushed candy canes). The Italians, however, enjoy this flavor as is, and I love the simplicity of it.

In honor of the Italian tradition, I've created an easy-to-make recipe using a peppermint extract. Look for a strong and high-quality peppermint extract. I used an organic peppermint extract by Flavorganics (www.flavorganics.com). I have also added salt to this recipe to help round out the flavor and give the Menta gelato a little salty kick at the finish.

Ingredients

1.6 ounces / 46 grams milk powder

6.35 ounces / 180 grams granulated sugar

1 pinch kosher salt

0.7 ounce / 20 grams tapioca starch

6.75 ounces / 192 grams heavy cream

24.15 ounces / 685 grams whole milk

0.9 ounce / 25 grams light corn syrup

0.3 ounce / 8 grams peppermint extract

Yield: About 1.5 quarts / 1.42 liters

Prepare

1. Mix the milk powder, sugar, salt, and tapioca starch in a bowl.
2. Add the heavy cream and whole milk and whisk well to incorporate all of the dry ingredients into the liquid.
3. Whisk in the corn syrup and peppermint extract.

Cook

4. Pour the mixture into a 2.5-quart / 2.36-liter saucepan, using a spatula to scrape the sides of the bowl. Place the saucepan on medium-high heat and cook, whisking continuously to prevent any burning or clumping. Whisk slowly in the beginning and increase speed as the mixture gets warmer and begins to steam and thicken. It should thicken without boiling after 8 to 12 minutes on the heat; watch carefully so it doesn't burn. Once the mixture has thickened enough to coat the back of a spoon, continue cooking 15 seconds longer, whisking vigorously. Then immediately remove from the heat.

Freeze

5. Pour the mixture into a clean glass or stainless-steel bowl and lay plastic wrap directly on the surface to prevent a skin from forming on top. Allow the mixture to sit 30 to 45 minutes, until no longer hot. Then place in the refrigerator to cool completely, about 4 hours. If the mixture needs to be used right away, submerge most of the bowl in an ice bath and let it sit 30 to 40 minutes, refreshing the ice as necessary.
6. Once the mixture has cooled completely and thickened further, pour it into the bowl of the gelato machine and churn the gelato according to the manufacturer's directions. The gelato will expand and should spin until it's thick and creamy but still soft enough to scoop into a storage container, about 30 to 55 minutes.
7. Using a rubber spatula, scoop the gelato into a storage container.
8. Press a piece of plastic wrap or parchment paper directly on the surface of the gelato, seal the container with an airtight lid, and put it in the freezer.
9. Freeze at least 4 to 5 hours. When ready, the gelato should be firm enough to scoop but soft and creamy in texture.

Serve

10. Enjoy the fresh gelato as soon as possible. If using after 1 day, allow 7 to 10 minutes for the gelato to soften outside of the freezer before eating.

OLIO D'OLIVA
Olive Oil

Olive oil may seem like a strange flavor for gelato, but Olio d'Oliva is common in Italy and becoming more popular throughout America as chefs blur the lines between savory and sweet. Olive oil is not necessarily savory, however. Good olive oil straight from an artisanal producer can have aromatic notes of flowers, fruit, or even herbs.

Pruneti, a Tuscan producer of olive oil, is my preferred source for this ingredient and has been for years. This purveyor makes some of the best olive oil I've ever had.

Ingredients

2 ounces / 56 grams milk powder

7.05 ounces / 200 grams granulated sugar

0.7 ounce / 20 grams tapioca starch

6.75 ounces / 192 grams heavy cream

24.15 ounces / 685 grams whole milk

1.15 ounces / 33 grams light corn syrup

1.25 ounces / 35 grams high-quality olive oil

Yield: About 1.5 quarts / 1.42 liters

Prepare

1. Mix the milk powder, sugar, and tapioca starch in a bowl.

2. Add the heavy cream and whole milk and whisk well to incorporate all of the dry ingredients into the liquid.

3. Whisk in the corn syrup.

Cook

4. Pour the mixture into a 2.5-quart / 2.36-liter saucepan, using a spatula to scrape the sides of the bowl. Place the saucepan on medium-high heat and cook, whisking continuously to prevent any burning or clumping. Whisk slowly in the beginning and increase speed as the mixture gets warmer and begins to steam and thicken. It should thicken without boiling after 8 to 12 minutes on the heat; watch carefully so it doesn't burn. Once the mixture has thickened enough to coat the back of a spoon, continue cooking 15 seconds longer, whisking vigorously. Then immediately remove from the heat.

Freeze

5. Pour the mixture into a clean glass or stainless-steel bowl and lay plastic wrap directly on the surface to prevent a skin from forming on top. Allow the mixture to sit 30 to 45 minutes, until no longer hot. Then place in the refrigerator to cool completely, about 4 hours. If the mixture needs to be used right away, submerge most of the bowl in an ice bath and let it sit 30 to 40 minutes, refreshing the ice as necessary.

6. Once the mixture has cooled completely and thickened further, pour it into the bowl of the gelato machine and churn the gelato according to the manufacturer's directions. About halfway through spinning, once the gelato has begun to thicken, pour the olive oil into the gelato as it spins, allowing the gelato paddle to incorporate the oil. (If it's not possible to pour in the olive oil while your machine is spinning, stop the machine, add the oil, and then start it again.) The gelato will continue to expand and should spin until it's thick and creamy but still soft enough to scoop into a storage container, about 30 to 55 minutes.

7. Using a rubber spatula, scoop the gelato into a storage container.

8. Press a piece of plastic wrap or parchment paper directly on the surface of the gelato, seal the container with an airtight lid, and put it in the freezer.

9. Freeze at least 4 to 5 hours. When ready, the gelato should be firm enough to scoop but soft and creamy in texture.

Serve

10. Enjoy the fresh gelato as soon as possible. If using after 1 day, allow 8 to 12 minutes for the gelato to soften outside of the freezer before eating.

RISO
Rice

Riso gelato is a flavor that many are hesitant to try and are pleasantly surprised after the first bite. It's a common flavor in Italy and loved by many, but those who are unfamiliar with it should think of Riso gelato as a frozen version of a creamy vanilla rice pudding. If rice pudding has never been your dessert of choice, then Riso may not be the gelato for you. But if you're already a rice-pudding lover or just want to surprise your guests with something new, give this flavor a try.

For a creamier rice base, try substituting instant rice for half of the cooked rice. Cook the instant rice in the base on the stovetop when thickening the starch. Just make sure the rice is fully cooked before cooling and freezing the gelato.

Ingredients

2 ounces / 56 grams milk powder

6.35 ounces / 180 grams granulated sugar

0.7 ounce / 20 grams tapioca starch

6.75 ounces / 192 grams heavy cream

24.15 ounces / 685 grams whole milk

0.2 ounce / 6 grams vanilla extract

1.15 ounces / 33 grams light corn syrup

4.35 ounces / 125 grams cooked medium- or long-grain rice, finely chopped

Yield: About 1.5 quarts / 1.42 liters

Prepare

1. Mix the milk powder, sugar, and tapioca starch in a bowl.

2. Add the heavy cream, whole milk, and vanilla extract and whisk well to incorporate all of the dry ingredients into the liquid.

3. Add the corn syrup and cooked rice. Blend with an immersion blender, making sure to reduce the rice to small pieces.

Cook

4. Pour the mixture into a 2.5-quart / 2.36-liter saucepan, using a spatula to scrape the sides of the bowl. Place the saucepan on medium-high heat and cook, whisking continuously to prevent any burning or clumping. Whisk slowly in the beginning and increase speed as the mixture gets warmer and begins to steam and thicken. It should thicken without boiling after 8 to 12 minutes on the heat; watch carefully so it doesn't burn. Once the mixture has thickened enough to coat the back of a spoon, continue cooking 15 seconds longer, whisking vigorously. Then immediately remove from the heat.

Freeze

5. Pour the mixture into a clean glass or stainless-steel bowl and lay plastic wrap directly on the surface to prevent a skin from forming on top. Allow the mixture to sit 30 to 45 minutes, until no longer hot. Then place in the refrigerator to cool completely, about 4 hours. If the mixture needs to be used right away, submerge most of the bowl in an ice bath and let it sit 30 to 40 minutes, refreshing the ice as necessary.

6. Once the mixture has cooled completely and thickened further, pour it into the bowl of the gelato machine and churn the gelato according to the manufacturer's directions. The gelato will expand and should spin until it's thick and creamy but still soft enough to scoop into a storage container, about 30 to 55 minutes.

7. Using a rubber spatula, scoop the gelato into a storage container.

8. Press a piece of plastic wrap or parchment paper directly on the surface of the gelato, seal the container with an airtight lid, and put it in the freezer.

9. Freeze at least 4 to 5 hours. When ready, the gelato should be firm enough to scoop but soft and creamy in texture.

Serve

10. Enjoy the fresh gelato as soon as possible. If using after 1 day, allow 10 to 12 minutes for the gelato to soften outside of the freezer before eating.

RICOTTA E PERA
Ricotta and Pear

Ricotta e Pera gelato is meant to mimic the creamy, pear-infused filling of one of the best and most popular Italian cakes, Torta Ricotta e Pere. In fact, Ricotta and Pear is one of my favorite flavors because of its sweetness and its texture. You can taste the ricotta, and the pears add a subtle dimension that contributes to the sweetness of the flavor.

I suggest using Bosc pears for this flavor since they ripen nicely and are usually juicier than other pears.

Due to Ricotta e Pera gelato's delicate flavor, I recommend it be enjoyed all on its own or perhaps as a complement to a simple, buttery piece of pound cake.

Ingredients

2 ounces / 56 grams milk powder

8 ounces / 225 grams granulated sugar

1 pinch kosher salt

0.7 ounce / 20 grams tapioca starch

7.1 ounces / 200 grams heavy cream

21.15 ounces / 600 grams whole milk

1.25 ounces / 36 grams light corn syrup

3.55 ounces / 100 grams whole cow's-milk ricotta

7.05 ounces / 200 grams ripe Bosc pears, peeled, ends removed, cored and diced (about 2 pears)

Yield: About 1.5 quarts / 1.42 liters

Prepare

1. Mix the milk powder, sugar, salt, and tapioca starch in a small bowl.
2. Add the heavy cream and whole milk and whisk well to incorporate all of the dry ingredients into the liquid.
3. Add the corn syrup, ricotta, and pear. Blend well with an immersion blender to incorporate all of the ingredients into the base, making sure the pear has been reduced to very fine pieces.

Cook

4. Pour the mixture into a 2.5-quart / 2.36-liter saucepan, using a spatula to scrape the sides of the bowl. Place the saucepan on medium-high heat and cook, whisking continuously to prevent any burning or clumping. Whisk slowly in the beginning and increase speed as the mixture gets warmer and begins to steam and thicken. It should thicken without boiling after 8 to 12 minutes on the heat; watch carefully so it doesn't burn. Once the mixture has thickened enough to coat the back of a spoon, continue cooking 15 seconds longer, whisking vigorously. Then immediately remove from the heat.

Freeze

5. Pour the mixture into a clean glass or stainless-steel bowl and lay plastic wrap directly on the surface to prevent a skin from forming on top. Allow the mixture

to sit 30 to 45 minutes, until no longer hot. Then place in the refrigerator to cool completely, about 4 hours. If the mixture needs to be used right away, submerge most of the bowl in an ice bath and let it sit 30 to 40 minutes, refreshing the ice as necessary.

6. Once the mixture has cooled completely and thickened further, pour it into the bowl of the gelato machine and churn the gelato according to the manufacturer's directions. The gelato will expand and should spin until it's thick and creamy but still soft enough to scoop into a storage container, about 30 to 55 minutes.

7. Using a rubber spatula, scoop the gelato into a storage container.

8. Press a piece of plastic wrap or parchment paper directly on the surface of the gelato, seal the container with an airtight lid, and put it in the freezer.

9. Freeze at least 4 to 5 hours. When ready, the gelato should be firm enough to scoop but soft and creamy in texture.

Serve

10. Enjoy the fresh gelato as soon as possible. If using after 1 day, allow 7 to 10 minutes for the gelato to soften outside of the freezer before eating.

Ricotta

Whole cow's-milk ricotta is a must for this recipe because of the fat content. I strongly suggest using the best and freshest ricotta possible as it will contribute to the gelato's depth of flavor. If it's available in your supermarket, I recommend ricotta from Calabro Cheese (www.calabrocheese.com). It's my favorite choice.

TIRAMISU
Tiramisu

Tiramisu, literally translated as "pick me up," is a popular Italian dessert featuring espresso, an egg-based custard, mascarpone, ladyfingers, Marsala wine, and a little chocolate. This gelato recipe has many of those essential ingredients, giving it a flavor profile very similar to the dessert.

Ingredients

2 ounces / 56 grams milk powder

6.35 ounces / 180 grams granulated sugar

0.7 ounce / 20 grams tapioca starch

7.6 ounces / 215 grams heavy cream

21.15 ounces / 600 grams whole milk

0.4 ounce / 12 grams sweet Marsala wine

1.15 ounces / 33 grams light corn syrup

Yield: About 1.5 quarts / 1.42 liters

3 ounces / 85 grams brewed and cooled espresso (just over 1 shot)

2 egg yolks

1.75 ounces / 60 grams 60% to 70% dark chocolate, finely chopped

1.4 ounces / 40 grams ladyfingers, crushed or finely chopped

Prepare

1. Mix the milk powder, sugar, and tapioca starch in a bowl.

2. Add the heavy cream, whole milk, and Marsala wine and whisk well to incorporate all of the dry ingredients into the liquid.

3. Whisk in the corn syrup, espresso, and egg yolks.

Cook

4. Pour the mixture into a 2.5-quart / 2.36-liter saucepan, using a spatula to scrape the sides of the bowl. Place the saucepan on medium-high heat and cook, whisking continuously to prevent any burning or clumping. Whisk slowly in the beginning and increase speed as the mixture gets warmer and begins to steam and thicken. It should thicken without boiling after 8 to 12 minutes on the heat; watch carefully so it doesn't burn. Once the mixture has thickened enough to coat the back of a spoon, continue cooking 15 seconds longer, whisking vigorously. Then immediately remove from the heat.

Freeze

5. Pour the mixture into a clean glass or stainless-steel bowl and lay plastic wrap directly on the surface to prevent a skin from forming on top. Allow the mixture to sit 30 to 45 minutes, until no longer hot. Then place in the refrigerator to cool completely, about 4 hours. If the mixture needs to be used right away, submerge most of the bowl in an ice bath and let it sit 30 to 40 minutes, refreshing the ice as necessary.

6. Once the mixture has cooled completely and thickened further, pour it into the bowl of the gelato machine, gently stir in the dark chocolate and ladyfingers, and churn the gelato according to the manufacturer's directions. The gelato will expand and should spin until it's thick and creamy but still soft enough to scoop into a storage container, about 30 to 55 minutes.

7. Using a rubber spatula, scoop the gelato into a storage container.

8. Press a piece of plastic wrap or parchment paper directly on the surface of the gelato, seal the container with an airtight lid, and put it in the freezer.

9. Freeze at least 4 to 5 hours. When ready, the gelato should be firm enough to scoop but soft and creamy in texture.

Serve

10. Enjoy the fresh gelato as soon as possible. If using after 1 day, allow 7 to 10 minutes for the gelato to soften outside of the freezer before eating.

ZABAIONE
Sweet Wine Custard

Zabaione is a classic dessert popular in many countries but with origins in Italy. It consists of egg yolks whipped well with sugar and a fortified wine to create a light and creamy custard, which is usually topped with berries and served in a champagne glass. It's one of my favorite desserts, and when mascarpone and espresso are added, I often use it as the base for my homemade tiramisu. Zabaione gelato may not have the same aerated texture as its dessert counterpart, but sugar, egg yolks, and wine are still used to create a delicious, creamy, and elegant gelato flavor. I recommend using a good-quality port for this recipe.

Zabaione gelato, like the dessert, is best enjoyed with blueberries, strawberries, raspberries, or any other kind of berry or fruit, or just by itself with a little whipped cream. For the best complementary garnish, use fresh, ripe fruit. Break out the champagne glasses and enjoy!

Ingredients

1.6 ounces / 46 grams milk powder

7.6 ounces / 215 grams granulated sugar

1 pinch kosher salt

0.7 ounce / 20 grams tapioca starch

8.8 ounces / 250 grams heavy cream

21.15 ounces / 600 grams whole milk

1.3 ounces / 37 grams port or other fortified wine

1.15 ounces / 33 grams light corn syrup

4 egg yolks

Assorted berries and mint leaves for garnish

Yield: About 1.5 quarts / 1.42 liters

Prepare

1. Mix the milk powder, sugar, salt, and tapioca starch in a bowl.
2. Add the heavy cream, whole milk, and wine and whisk well to incorporate all of the dry ingredients into the liquid.
3. Whisk in the corn syrup and egg yolks.

Cook

4. Pour the mixture into a 2.5-quart / 2.36-liter saucepan, using a spatula to scrape the sides of the bowl. Place the saucepan on medium-high heat and cook, whisking continuously to prevent any burning or clumping. Whisk slowly in the beginning and increase speed as the mixture gets warmer and begins to steam and thicken. It should thicken without boiling after 8 to 12 minutes on the heat; watch carefully so it doesn't burn. Once the mixture has thickened enough to coat the back of a spoon, continue cooking 15 seconds longer, whisking vigorously. Then immediately remove from the heat.

Freeze

5. Pour the mixture into a clean glass or stainless-steel bowl and lay plastic wrap directly on the surface to prevent a skin from forming on top. Allow the mixture to sit 30 to 45 minutes, until no longer hot. Then place in the refrigerator to cool completely, about 4 hours. If the mixture needs to be used right away, submerge most of the bowl in an ice bath and let it sit 30 to 40 minutes, refreshing the ice as necessary.

6. Once the mixture has cooled completely and thickened further, pour it into the bowl of the gelato machine and churn the gelato according to the manufacturer's directions. The gelato will expand and should spin until it's thick and creamy but still soft enough to scoop into a storage container, about 30 to 55 minutes.

7. Using a rubber spatula, scoop the gelato into a storage container.

8. Press a piece of plastic wrap or parchment paper directly on the surface of the gelato, seal the container with an airtight lid, and put it in the freezer.

9. Freeze at least 4 to 5 hours. When ready, the gelato should be firm enough to scoop but soft and creamy in texture.

Serve

10. Enjoy the fresh gelato as soon as possible. If using after 1 day, allow 7 to 10 minutes for the gelato to soften outside of the freezer before eating. Garnish with berries and mint leaves, as desired.

Fortified Wine

A fortified wine like port is one to which additional alcohol has been added during the fermentation process. Fortified wines are usually viscous and on the sweet side. Other fortified wines include sherry, Marsala, and Madeira. Your gelato will take on slightly different flavors depending on the wine you choose. Experiment to find your favorite.

CREMA FIORENTINA
Florentine Cream

Based on Florence's gelateria Badiani's famous Buontalenti gelato, Crema Fiorentina, with its hints of vanilla, egg, and orange, is touted as the city's signature flavor. Bernardo Buontalenti, a multitalented Florentine man, is credited as the inventor of modern gelato. Buontalenti introduced his own gelato recipe and hand-cranked machine to the Medici, Florence's ruling family, at a large banquet in the sixteenth century. They were so impressed that the rest, as we say, is history. Many variations have sprung up over the years—here's ours for you to try. For a fun twist, try folding equal parts homemade whipped cream into the gelato once it has had time to set in the freezer but is still soft in consistency. It will produce a cold, mousse-like dessert.

Crema Fiorentina is a great alternative to Crema all'Uovo (page 34) and can be paired with almost any other gelato or sorbet flavor. Flecked with vanilla seeds, orange zest, and a hint of salt, Crema Fiorentina gelato will delight the palate and is sure to be a hit at any summer dinner party.

Ingredients

1.6 ounces / 46 grams milk powder

7.6 ounces / 215 grams granulated sugar

1 pinch kosher salt

0.7 ounce / 20 grams tapioca starch

8.8 ounces / 250 grams heavy cream

21.15 ounces / 600 grams whole milk

1.15 ounces / 33 grams light corn syrup

4 egg yolks

1 vanilla bean, sliced down the middle and opened, seeds scraped out

Zest of 1/2 orange, finely chopped

Yield: About 1.5 quarts / 1.42 liters

Prepare

1. Mix the milk powder, sugar, salt, and tapioca starch in a bowl.
2. Add the heavy cream and whole milk and whisk well to incorporate all of the dry ingredients into the liquid.
3. Whisk in the corn syrup and egg yolks.

Cook

4. Pour the mixture into a 2.5-quart / 2.36-liter saucepan, using a spatula to scrape the sides of the bowl. Whisk in the vanilla bean seeds. Place the saucepan on medium-high heat and cook, whisking continuously to prevent any burning or clumping. Whisk slowly in the beginning and increase speed as the mixture gets warmer and begins to steam and thicken. It should thicken without boiling after 8 to 12 minutes on the heat; watch carefully so it doesn't burn. Once the mixture has thickened enough to coat the back of a spoon, continue cooking 15 seconds longer, whisking vigorously. Then immediately remove from the heat.

Freeze

5. Pour the mixture into a clean glass or stainless-steel bowl and lay plastic wrap directly on the surface to prevent a skin from forming on top. Allow the mixture to sit 30 to 45 minutes, until no longer hot. Then place in the refrigerator to cool completely, about 4 hours. If the mixture needs to be used right away, submerge most of the bowl in an ice bath and let it sit 30 to 40 minutes, refreshing the ice as necessary.

6. Once the mixture has cooled completely and thickened further, whisk in the orange zest, pour the mixture into the bowl of the gelato machine, and churn according to the manufacturer's directions. The gelato will expand and should spin until it's thick and creamy but still soft enough to scoop into a storage container, about 30 to 55 minutes.

7. Using a rubber spatula, scoop the gelato into a storage container.

8. Press a piece of plastic wrap or parchment paper directly on the surface of the gelato, seal the container with an airtight lid, and put it in the freezer.

9. Freeze at least 4 to 5 hours. When ready, the gelato should be firm enough to scoop but soft and creamy in texture.

Serve

10. Enjoy the fresh gelato as soon as possible. If using after 1 day, allow 7 to 10 minutes for the gelato to soften outside of the freezer before eating.

Oranges and Zest

The easiest and most efficient way to get the zest you need from the orange is by using a microplane. The teeth are much sharper and more even than the smallest holes in a traditional grater. Make sure you only take the zest from the very top layer of the skin. The white pith beneath the skin is bitter and should be avoided when zesting.

CREMA CATALANA
Crème Brûlée

Crema Catalana is a fun and unique flavor to make, particularly for those who love crème brûlée as a dessert. Crema Catalana gets its name from the Spanish version of crème brûlée and is a common gelato flavor in Italy, usually without the caramelized sugar on top. Considering that's my favorite part of the dessert, I have included the crunchy sugar topping in this recipe.

Although it requires additional time to prep, Crema Catalana is well worth it. I recommend making this gelato the night before you plan to serve it so the gelato can firm up in the freezer overnight. A small brûlée torch is required, and I recommend using a high-quality vanilla extract, such as a brand of Madagascar vanilla, which should be available in the baking aisle of most supermarkets. A small, quart-sized glass storage container is also necessary for the gelato when caramelizing the sugar on top.

Crema Catalana should wow any dinner guest and is best served by itself in its glass dish.

Ingredients

1.6 ounces / 46 grams milk powder

7.6 ounces / 215 grams granulated sugar

1 pinch kosher salt

0.7 ounce / 20 grams tapioca starch

8.8 ounces / 250 grams heavy cream

21.15 ounces / 600 grams whole milk

0.18 ounces / 5 grams vanilla extract

1.15 ounces / 33 grams light corn syrup

4 egg yolks

1 vanilla bean, sliced down the middle and opened, seeds scraped out

Granulated sugar, for caramelizing

Yield: About 1.5 quarts / 1.42 liters

Prepare

1. Mix the milk powder, sugar, salt, and tapioca starch in a bowl.
2. Add the heavy cream, whole milk, and vanilla extract and whisk well to incorporate all of the dry ingredients into the liquid.
3. Whisk in the corn syrup and egg yolks.

Cook

4. Pour the mixture into a 2.5-quart / 2.36-liter saucepan, using a spatula to scrape the sides of the bowl. Whisk in the vanilla bean seeds. Place the saucepan on medium-high heat and cook, whisking continuously to prevent any burning or clumping. Whisk slowly in the beginning and increase speed as the mixture gets warmer and begins to steam and thicken. It should thicken without boiling after 8 to 12 minutes on the heat; watch carefully so it doesn't burn. Once the mixture has thickened enough to coat the back of a spoon, continue cooking 15 seconds longer, whisking vigorously. Then immediately remove from the heat.

Freeze

5. Pour the mixture into a clean glass or stainless-steel bowl and lay plastic wrap directly on the surface to prevent a skin from forming on top. Allow the mixture to sit 30 to 45 minutes, until no longer hot. Then place in the refrigerator to cool completely, about 4 hours. If the mixture needs to be used right away, submerge most of the bowl in an ice bath and let it sit 30 to 40 minutes, refreshing the ice as necessary.

6. Once the mixture has cooled completely and thickened further, pour it into the bowl of the gelato machine and churn the gelato according to the manufacturer's directions. The gelato will expand and should spin until it's thick and creamy but still soft enough to scoop into a storage container, about 30 to 55 minutes.

7. Using a rubber spatula, scoop the gelato into a glass storage container that would be appropriate for serving. Make sure it is evenly distributed in the container and then smooth out the gelato's surface as much as possible.

8. Press a piece of plastic wrap or parchment paper directly on the surface of the gelato, seal with an airtight lid, and place in the freezer.

9. Freeze until very firm, at least 10 hours. After 10 hours, pull the gelato from the freezer, remove the parchment paper or plastic wrap, and use a spatula or other utensil to smooth out the surface of the gelato one more time. Place the gelato back in the freezer for another 10 minutes while you prepare the torch.

Brûlée

10. Sprinkle enough sugar on the gelato to cover the surface. Pick up the dish and lightly tilt it in all directions so that the sugar coats the entire surface. With the torch flame setting on medium-low, slowly heat the surface, lightly caramelizing the first layer of sugar. Spend no more than 5 minutes going over the entire surface and then return the gelato, uncovered, to the freezer for 20 minutes. It's important to work as quickly as possible to ensure that the gelato does not melt. Add a second coat of sugar to the surface of the gelato and repeat the caramelizing process two more times, browning the last layer of sugar as much as possible. The last layer may take a little more time to get the sugar to caramelize and fully change color.

11. Place the gelato in the freezer one last time for about an hour to allow the surface of the gelato to freeze, and then Crema Catalana is ready to be served.

Serve

12. Enjoy the fresh gelato as soon as possible. If using after 1 day, allow 8 to 12 minutes for the gelato to soften outside of the freezer before eating.

NOCI
Nuts

MANDORLA
Almond

Mandorla will be a hit with anyone who is a fan of almonds or marzipan. It's loaded with flavor, sweet with a slight salty finish, and has plenty of crushed almonds for texture. Sicily is known for its almonds—if you can get your hands on a bag of those, use them in this recipe. Alternatively, California produces great almonds that will work in this recipe as well. You'd be surprised at how different the gelato tastes when it's made with strong-flavored and high-quality almonds.

Almond gelato is often eaten alone or paired with Dark Chocolate (page 48), although I've made many frappés of this flavor for those customers who cannot get enough of it. For a little extra crunch, especially for the almond lover, toast a handful of almonds. After they cool, chop them finely, sprinkle them on top of a bowl of Mandorla, and finish with a light dusting of sea salt flakes. This garnish, I promise, will not disappoint.

Ingredients

1.6 ounces / 46 grams milk powder

6.35 ounces / 180 grams granulated sugar

2 pinches kosher salt

0.7 ounce / 20 grams tapioca starch

6.75 ounces / 192 grams heavy cream

24.15 ounces / 685 grams whole milk

1.15 ounces / 33 grams light corn syrup

0.2 ounce / 5 grams almond extract

2.45 ounces / 70 grams almonds, shelled and roughly chopped with skins on, plus additional chopped almonds for garnish (optional)

Yield: About 1.5 quarts / 1.42 liters

Prepare

1. Mix the milk powder, sugar, salt, and tapioca starch in a bowl.
2. Add the heavy cream and whole milk and whisk well to incorporate all of the dry ingredients into the liquid.
3. Add the corn syrup, almond extract, and almonds. Blend with an immersion blender to fully incorporate the ingredients, making sure the almonds are reduced to small pieces.

Cook

4. Pour the mixture into a 2.5-quart / 2.36-liter saucepan, using a spatula to scrape the sides of the bowl. Place the saucepan on medium-high heat and cook, whisking continuously to prevent any burning or clumping. Whisk slowly in the beginning and increase speed as the mixture gets warmer and begins to steam and thicken. It should thicken without boiling after 8 to 12 minutes on the heat; watch carefully so it doesn't burn. Once the mixture has thickened enough to coat the back of a spoon, continue cooking 15 seconds longer, whisking vigorously. Then immediately remove from the heat.

Tip

The secret to getting the maximum depth and breadth of flavor for Almond gelato is to use more than one form of the nut. Using a good-quality almond extract is essential. Also, leaving the skins on the almonds gives both additional flavor and color.

Freeze

5. Pour the mixture into a clean glass or stainless-steel bowl and lay plastic wrap directly on the surface to prevent a skin from forming on top. Allow the mixture to sit 30 to 45 minutes, until no longer hot. Then place in the refrigerator to cool completely, about 4 hours. If the mixture needs to be used right away, submerge most of the bowl in an ice bath and let it sit 30 to 40 minutes, refreshing the ice as necessary.

6. Once the mixture has cooled completely and thickened further, pour it into the bowl of the gelato machine and churn the gelato according to the manufacturer's directions. The gelato will expand and should spin until it's thick and creamy but still soft enough to scoop into a storage container, about 30 to 55 minutes.

7. Using a rubber spatula, scoop the gelato into a storage container.

8. Press a piece of plastic wrap or parchment paper directly on the surface of the gelato, seal the container with an airtight lid, and put it in the freezer.

9. Freeze at least 4 to 5 hours. When ready, the gelato should be firm enough to scoop but soft and creamy in texture.

Serve

10. Enjoy the fresh gelato as soon as possible. If using after 1 day, allow 8 to 12 minutes for the gelato to soften outside of the freezer before eating. Garnish with chopped almonds before serving, if desired.

Try it Affrogato Style

For a sweet way to kick-start your day, enjoy Mandorla gelato the way Italians do—affrogato al caffè, or literally, "drowned in coffee." Start with a scoop of the gelato and pour a shot of espresso over the top of it.

MANDORLA E ARANCIA
Almond and Orange

Citrus zest adds a fun flavor twist to Almond gelato, giving a new dimension to the taste. The orange flavor makes the gelato all the more refreshing on a hot day.

Enjoy this gelato alone or paired with a complementary dessert, such as a simple Italian crostata or a buttery cake. Mandorla e Arancia is a not-to-miss flavor that offers a pleasant surprise to the taste buds.

Ingredients

1.6 ounces / 46 grams milk powder

6.35 ounces / 180 grams granulated sugar

2 pinches kosher salt

0.7 ounce / 20 grams tapioca starch

6.75 ounces / 192 grams heavy cream

24.15 ounces / 685 grams whole milk

1.15 ounces / 33 grams light corn syrup

0.2 ounce / 5 grams almond extract

2.45 ounces / 70 grams almonds, shelled and roughly chopped with skins on

Zest of 2 oranges, finely chopped

Yield: About 1.5 quarts / 1.42 liters

Prepare

1. Mix the milk powder, sugar, salt, and tapioca starch in a bowl.

2. Add the heavy cream and whole milk and whisk well to incorporate all of the dry ingredients into the liquid.

3. Add the corn syrup, almond extract, and almonds. Blend with an immersion blender to fully incorporate the ingredients, making sure the almonds are reduced to small pieces.

Cook

4. Pour the mixture into a 2.5-quart / 2.36-liter saucepan, using a spatula to scrape the sides of the bowl. Place the saucepan on medium-high heat and cook, whisking continuously to prevent any burning or clumping. Whisk slowly in the beginning and increase speed as the mixture gets warmer and begins to steam and thicken. It should thicken without boiling after 8 to 12 minutes on the heat; watch carefully so it doesn't burn. Once the mixture has thickened enough to coat the back of a spoon, continue cooking 15 seconds longer, whisking vigorously. Then immediately remove from the heat.

Freeze

5. Pour the mixture into a clean glass or stainless-steel bowl, whisk in the orange zest, and then lay plastic wrap directly on the surface of the mixture to prevent a skin from forming on top. Allow the base to sit 30 to 45 minutes, until no longer hot. Then place in the refrigerator to cool completely, about 4 hours. If the mixture needs to be used right away, submerge most of the bowl in an ice bath and let it sit 30 to 40 minutes, refreshing the ice as necessary.

6. Once the mixture has cooled completely and thickened further, pour it into the bowl of the gelato machine and churn the gelato according to the manufacturer's directions. The gelato will expand and should spin until it's thick and creamy but still soft enough to scoop into a storage container, about 30 to 55 minutes.

7. Using a rubber spatula, scoop the gelato into a storage container.

8. Press a piece of plastic wrap or parchment paper directly on the surface of the gelato, seal the container with an airtight lid, and put it in the freezer.

9. Freeze at least 4 to 5 hours. When ready, the gelato should be firm enough to scoop but soft and creamy in texture.

Serve

10. Enjoy the fresh gelato as soon as possible. If using after 1 day, allow 8 to 12 minutes for the gelato to soften outside of the freezer before eating.

NOCCIOLA
Hazelnut

Nocciola, one of the most popular flavors at Morano Gelato Hanover, is even better than eating Nutella straight from the jar. That's partly because we get our hazelnuts from the same place as those used to make Nutella: the Piedmont region of Italy, which is renowned for this nut.

If a ground hazelnut paste from this region is not obtainable (and it is hard to get), the next best option is the hazelnut praline paste by Love'n Bake. Since it contains added sugar, like most other commercially available pastes, I've adjusted the recipe accordingly. If you use an unsweetened ground hazelnut paste, the recipe will require increasing the amount of granulated sugar by 20 percent. Although Morano Gelato's Hazelnut gelato does not contain nut pieces, I've added roasted chopped hazelnuts to this recipe to deepen the flavor. I've also added salt to give the gelato the savory profile it needs.

Enjoy Nocciola gelato as is, paired with a chocolate flavor, or with Crema all' Uovo (page 34) or Fior di Latte (page 30).

Ingredients

1.05 ounces / 30 grams milk powder

5.1 ounces / 144 grams granulated sugar

2 pinches kosher salt

0.6 ounce / 17 grams tapioca starch

5.45 ounces / 154 grams heavy cream

19.35 ounces / 548 grams whole milk

0.95 ounce / 27 grams light corn syrup

1.05 ounces / 30 grams surface oil from hazelnut praline paste (if the oil has been mixed into the paste, add this amount to the total hazelnut paste below)

2.8 ounces / 80 grams hazelnut praline paste, solid part only

1.6 ounces / 45 grams hazelnuts, roasted (see Roasting Hazelnuts, opposite page) and chopped

Yield: About 1.5 quarts / 1.42 liters

Prepare

1. Mix the milk powder, sugar, salt, and tapioca starch in a bowl.

2. Add the heavy cream and whole milk and whisk well to incorporate all of the dry ingredients into the liquid.

3. Add the corn syrup and hazelnut praline oil and paste. Blend with an immersion blender to fully incorporate the ingredients, making sure no large pieces of the hazelnut praline paste remain.

Cook

4. Pour the mixture into a 2.5-quart / 2.36-liter saucepan, using a spatula to scrape the sides of the bowl. Place the saucepan on medium-high heat and cook, whisking continuously to prevent any burning or clumping. Whisk slowly in the beginning and increase speed as the mixture gets warmer and begins to steam and thicken. It should thicken without boiling after 8 to 12 minutes on the heat; watch carefully so it doesn't burn. Once the mixture has thickened enough to coat the back of a spoon, continue cooking 15 seconds longer, whisking vigorously. Then immediately remove from the heat.

Freeze

5. Pour the mixture into a clean glass or stainless-steel bowl, whisk in the hazelnuts, and then lay plastic wrap directly on the surface of the mixture to prevent a skin from forming on top. Allow the base to sit 30 to 45 minutes, until no longer hot. Then place in the refrigerator to cool completely, about 4 hours. If the mixture needs to be used right away, submerge most of the bowl in an ice bath and let it sit 30 to 40 minutes, refreshing the ice as necessary.

6. Once the mixture has cooled completely and thickened further, pour it into the bowl of the gelato machine and churn the gelato according to the manufacturer's directions. The gelato will expand and should spin until it's thick and creamy but still soft enough to scoop into a storage container, about 30 to 55 minutes.

7. Using a rubber spatula, scoop the gelato into a storage container.

8. Press a piece of plastic wrap or parchment paper directly on the surface of the gelato, seal the container with an airtight lid, and put it in the freezer.

9. Freeze at least 4 to 5 hours. When ready, the gelato should be firm enough to scoop but soft and creamy in texture.

Serve

10. Enjoy the fresh gelato as soon as possible. If using after 1 day, allow 10 to 15 minutes for the gelato to soften outside of the freezer before eating.

Roasting Hazelnuts

Preheat the oven to 350 degrees F/ 177 degrees C.

Spread the hazelnuts on a baking sheet in an even layer and bake, checking after 10 minutes. If they are brown and smell nutty, remove the hazelnuts from the oven and allow them to cool. If they need more time, check every 2 minutes until they are fully toasted.

Make sure not to leave the hazelnuts in the oven too long. Over-roasting them results in bitter and bad-tasting hazelnuts.

PISTACCHIO
Pistachio

Pistachio ice cream is not always a popular choice. As a result, it's often flavored with a combination of almonds and pistachios, much to the distress of any true pistachio fan. Morano Gelato uses pistachios from the Bronte region of Sicily. These pistachios are famous for their vibrant green color and bold flavor. Bronte pistachios grow on the volcanic rocks of Sicily's Mount Etna, the largest active volcano in Italy and, while they are ubiquitous in culinary and dessert preparations in Sicily, they are rare outside the island.

That said, Bronte pistachios and their by-products are beginning to grow in popularity in the United States. If you're able to find 100 percent pure ground Bronte pistachios or pistachio paste, use them in this recipe. If not, I've found a good pistachio paste by Love'n Bake that works well combined with raw and shelled domestic pistachios.

If you're a diehard pistachio person, this flavor may be best served alone, but I've always enjoyed it with a little Cioccolato Fondente (page 48) or Fior di Latte (page 30) gelato.

Ingredients

1.05 ounces / 30 grams milk powder

5.1 ounces / 144 grams granulated sugar

2 pinches kosher salt

0.6 ounce / 17 grams tapioca starch

5.45 ounces / 154 grams heavy cream

19.35 ounces / 548 grams whole milk

0.95 ounce / 27 grams light corn syrup

1.4 ounces / 40 grams pistachio paste, solid part only, no oil

2.1 ounces / 60 grams raw pistachios, shelled and roughly chopped

Ground pistachios for garnish (optional)

Yield: About 1.5 quarts / 1.42 liters

Prepare

1. Mix the milk powder, sugar, salt, and tapioca starch in a bowl.
2. Add the heavy cream and whole milk and whisk well to incorporate all of the dry ingredients into the liquid.
3. Add the corn syrup, pistachio paste, and pistachios. Blend with an immersion blender to fully incorporate the ingredients, making sure no large pieces of the pistachio paste or pistachios remain. The finer the pieces of pistachio, the better.

Cook

4. Pour the mixture into a 2.5-quart / 2.36-liter saucepan, using a spatula to scrape the sides of the bowl. Place the saucepan on medium-high heat and cook, whisking continuously to prevent any burning or clumping. Whisk slowly in the beginning and increase speed as the mixture gets warmer and begins to steam and thicken. It should thicken without boiling after 8 to 12 minutes on the heat; watch carefully so it doesn't burn. Once the mixture has thickened enough to coat the back of a spoon, continue cooking 15 seconds longer, whisking vigorously. Then immediately remove from the heat.

Freeze

5. Pour the mixture into a clean glass or stainless-steel bowl and lay plastic wrap directly on the surface to prevent a skin from forming on top. Allow the mixture to sit 30 to 45 minutes, until no longer hot. Then place in the refrigerator to cool completely, about 4 hours. If the mixture needs

to be used right away, submerge most of the bowl in an ice bath and let it sit 30 to 40 minutes, refreshing the ice as necessary.

6. Once the mixture has cooled completely and thickened further, pour it into the bowl of the gelato machine and churn the gelato according to the manufacturer's directions. The gelato will expand and should spin until it's thick and creamy but still soft enough to scoop into a storage container, about 30 to 55 minutes.

7. Using a rubber spatula, scoop the gelato into a storage container.

8. Press a piece of plastic wrap or parchment paper directly on the surface of the gelato, seal the container with an airtight lid, and put it in the freezer.

9. Freeze at least 4 to 5 hours. When ready, the gelato should be firm enough to scoop but soft and creamy in texture.

Serve

10. Enjoy the fresh gelato as soon as possible. If using after 1 day, allow 7 to 10 minutes for the gelato to soften outside of the freezer before eating. Sprinkle with ground pistachios, if desired.

Pistachios

Bronte pistachios are only harvested every two years. Brontese farmers discovered that pistachio trees give a much higher yield and higher-quality nuts if allowed to skip a year. To this end, every other year, all the buds are snipped off the trees and no nuts are harvested.

NOCE
Walnut

Although Noce gelato is not very common in America, it's popular in Italy. For those who appreciate walnuts or are looking for a unique nut flavor, this is it.

Walnut is a particularly nice flavor in the winter months, paired with a warm dessert or as a cold topping for a fresh-out-of-the-oven batch of brownies.

Ingredients

1.6 ounces / 46 grams milk powder

7.05 ounces / 200 grams granulated sugar

2 pinches kosher salt

0.7 ounce / 20 grams tapioca starch

6.75 ounces / 192 grams heavy cream

24.15 ounces / 685 grams whole milk

1.27 ounces / 36 grams light corn syrup

4.75 ounces / 135 grams raw walnuts, shelled and roughly chopped

Yield: About 1.5 quarts / 1.42 liters

Prepare

1. Mix the milk powder, sugar, salt and tapioca starch in a bowl.

2. Add the heavy cream and whole milk and whisk well to incorporate all of the dry ingredients into the liquid.

3. Add the corn syrup and walnuts. Blend with an immersion blender to fully incorporate the ingredients, making sure the walnuts are broken down into little pieces.

Cook

4. Pour the mixture into a 2.5-quart / 2.36-liter saucepan, using a spatula to scrape the sides of the bowl. Place the saucepan on medium-high heat and cook, whisking continuously to prevent any burning or clumping. Whisk slowly in the beginning and increase speed as the mixture gets warmer and begins to steam and thicken. It should thicken without boiling after 8 to 12 minutes on the heat; watch carefully so it doesn't burn. Once the mixture has thickened enough to coat the back of a spoon, continue cooking 15 seconds longer, whisking vigorously. Then immediately remove from the heat.

Freeze

5. Pour the mixture into a clean glass or stainless-steel bowl and lay plastic wrap directly on the surface to prevent a skin from forming on top. Allow the mixture to sit 30 to 45 minutes, until no longer hot. Then place in the refrigerator to cool completely, about 4 hours. If the mixture needs to be used right away, submerge most of the bowl in an ice bath and let it sit 30 to 40 minutes, refreshing the ice as necessary.

6. Once the mixture has cooled completely and thickened further, pour it into the bowl of the gelato machine and churn the gelato according to the manufacturer's directions. The gelato will expand and should spin until it's thick and creamy but still soft enough to scoop into a storage container, about 30 to 55 minutes.

7. Using a rubber spatula, scoop the gelato into a storage container.

8. Press a piece of plastic wrap or parchment paper directly on the surface of the gelato, seal the container with an airtight lid, and put it in the freezer.

9. Freeze at least 4 to 5 hours. When ready, the gelato should be firm enough to scoop but soft and creamy in texture.

Serve

10. Enjoy the fresh gelato as soon as possible. If using after 1 day, allow 10 to 15 minutes for the gelato to soften outside of the freezer before eating.

PINOLO
Pine Nut

Pinolo gelato is an elegant dessert with a very Italian flavor profile. After all, rarely do you see a pine-nut ice cream in American ice cream parlors. This gelato is as buttery and rich as the pine nuts themselves, with a delicious creaminess.

For a variation of this recipe, try toasting the pine nuts until they're a dark brown to make a toasted pine-nut gelato. Just be careful when toasting the pine nuts—they brown quickly!

Ingredients

2 ounces / 56 grams milk powder

6.35 ounces / 180 grams granulated sugar

2 pinches kosher salt

0.7 ounce / 20 grams tapioca starch

6.75 ounces / 192 grams heavy cream

24.15 ounces / 685 grams whole milk

1.15 ounces / 33 grams light corn syrup

2.8 ounces / 80 grams whole pine nuts

Yield: About 1.5 quarts / 1.42 liters

Prepare

1. Mix the milk powder, sugar, salt, and tapioca starch in a bowl.

2. Add the heavy cream and whole milk and whisk well to incorporate all of the dry ingredients into the liquid.

3. Add the corn syrup and pine nuts. Blend with an immersion blender to fully incorporate the ingredients, making sure the pine nuts are reduced to small pieces.

Cook

4. Pour the mixture into a 2.5-quart / 2.36-liter saucepan, using a spatula to scrape the sides of the bowl. Place the saucepan on medium-high heat and cook, whisking continuously to prevent any burning or clumping. Whisk slowly in the beginning and increase speed as the mixture gets warmer and begins to steam and thicken. It should thicken without boiling after 8 to 12 minutes on the heat; watch carefully so it doesn't burn. Once the mixture has thickened enough to coat the back of a spoon, continue cooking 15 seconds longer, whisking vigorously. Then immediately remove from the heat.

Freeze

5. Pour the mixture into a clean glass or stainless-steel bowl and lay plastic wrap directly on the surface to prevent a skin from forming on top. Allow the mixture to sit 30 to 45 minutes, until no longer hot. Then place in the refrigerator to cool completely, about 4 hours. If the mixture needs to be used right away, submerge most of the bowl in an ice bath and let it sit 30 to 40 minutes, refreshing the ice as necessary.

6. Once the mixture has cooled completely and thickened further, pour it into the bowl of the gelato machine and churn the gelato according to the manufacturer's directions. The gelato will expand and should spin until it's thick and creamy but still soft enough to scoop into a storage container, about 30 to 55 minutes.

7. Using a rubber spatula, scoop the gelato into a storage container.

8. Press a piece of plastic wrap or parchment paper directly on the surface of the gelato, seal the container with an airtight lid, and put it in the freezer.

9. Freeze at least 4 to 5 hours. When ready, the gelato should be firm enough to scoop but soft and creamy in texture.

Serve

10. Enjoy the fresh gelato as soon as possible. If using after 1 day, allow 7 to 10 minutes for the gelato to soften outside of the freezer before eating.

NOCE E PERA
Walnut and Pear

A fun twist on the Noce (page 130) flavor, Noce e Pera is to the Italians what walnut and banana is to Americans. Since I've never been a huge fan of bananas, I'm much more partial to Walnut and Pear. The pear, although subtle, adds a new complexity while sweetening the gelato further than the original Walnut flavor. Bosc pears are my top choice because of their sweetness and soft texture. Be sure to choose pears at the peak of ripeness.

I recommend serving Walnut and Pear gelato by itself, but, like Noce gelato, it can be used to top warm desserts or even be paired with Crema all'Uovo (page 34) and Fior di Latte (page 30).

Ingredients

1.6 ounces / 46 grams milk powder

7.6 ounces / 215 grams granulated sugar

2 pinches kosher salt

0.7 ounce / 20 grams tapioca starch

6.75 ounces / 192 grams heavy cream

24.15 ounces / 685 grams whole milk

1.41 ounces / 40 grams light corn syrup

4.75 ounces / 135 grams raw walnuts, shelled and roughly chopped

6.5 ounces / 186 grams Bosc pear, peeled, ends removed, cored, and diced (about 2 pears)

Yield: About 1.5 quarts / 1.42 liters

Prepare

1. Mix the milk powder, sugar, salt and tapioca starch in a bowl.
2. Add the heavy cream and whole milk and whisk well to incorporate all of the dry ingredients into the liquid.
3. Add the corn syrup, walnuts, and pear. Blend with an immersion blender to incorporate the ingredients, making sure the walnuts are broken down into little pieces and the pear pieces are almost fully blended into the base.

Cook

4. Pour the mixture into a 2.5-quart / 2.36-liter saucepan, using a spatula to scrape the sides of the bowl. Place the saucepan on medium-high heat and cook, whisking continuously to prevent any burning or clumping. Whisk slowly in the beginning and increase speed as the mixture gets warmer and begins to steam and thicken. It should thicken without boiling after 8 to 12 minutes on the heat; watch carefully so it doesn't burn. Once the mixture has thickened enough to coat the back of a spoon, continue cooking 15 seconds longer, whisking vigorously. Then immediately remove from the heat.

Freeze

5. Pour the mixture into a clean glass or stainless-steel bowl and lay plastic wrap directly on the surface to prevent a skin from forming on top. Allow the mixture to sit 30 to 45 minutes, until no longer hot. Then place in the refrigerator to cool completely, about 4 hours. If the mixture needs to be used right away, submerge most of the bowl in an ice bath and let it sit 30 to 40 minutes, refreshing the ice as necessary.

6. Once the mixture has cooled completely and thickened further, pour it into the bowl of the gelato machine and churn the gelato according to the manufacturer's directions. The gelato will expand and should spin until it's thick and creamy but still soft enough to scoop into a storage container, about 30 to 55 minutes.

7. Using a rubber spatula, scoop the gelato into a storage container.

8. Press a piece of plastic wrap or parchment paper directly on the surface of the gelato, seal the container with an airtight lid, and put it in the freezer.

9. Freeze at least 4 to 5 hours. When ready, the gelato should be firm enough to scoop but soft and creamy in texture.

Serve

10. Enjoy the fresh gelato as soon as possible. If using after 1 day, allow 12 to 15 minutes for the gelato to soften outside of the freezer before eating.

Raw Walnuts

Raw walnuts, those that are not roasted, irradiated, or pastuerized, are called for in this gelato recipe. For maximum health benefits, leave on the skins, which contain up to 90 percent of the antioxidants.

NON TRADIZIONALE
Nontraditional

TORTA DI MELE
Apple Pie

At Morano Gelato, this is a one-day-only flavor, made on the Fourth of July. It's the only time that American flavors take precedence over Italian in the gelateria. I remember planning the flavors in advance for the first Fourth of July at what is now Morano Gelato Hanover. I knew Apple Pie had to be one of them, and I knew it would surprise and delight our customers. Eating apple pie in frozen form may seem unusual, but the gelato is delicious, very popular, and extremely easy to make.

In New Hampshire, we're fortunate enough to be surrounded by many apple orchards that produce very flavorful fruit. These apples are used to make some of the best apple pies I've had, particularly those from Lou's Bakery, which is just across the street from Morano Gelato Hanover. Their pie served as inspiration when I first made this gelato flavor in 2011—and since then, I've never looked back! Torta di Mele is pure comfort, from its bits of cooked apples to its flecks of cinnamon, and is sure to be enjoyed by all who try it.

Apple Pie gelato is a great alternative to pie and is perfect in the fall when apples are at their peak. Try it blended with milk in a frappé (page 51) and topped with whipped cream—it may become your new dessert of choice.

Ingredients

2 ounces / 56 grams milk powder

7.05 ounces / 200 grams granulated sugar

1 pinch kosher salt

1 pinch ground cinnamon

0.7 ounce / 20 grams tapioca starch

6.75 ounces / 192 grams heavy cream

24.15 ounces / 685 grams whole milk

1.15 ounces / 33 grams light corn syrup

7.05 ounces / 200 grams apple pie filling

Yield: About 1.5 quarts / 1.42 liters

Prepare

1. Mix the milk powder, sugar, salt, cinnamon, and tapioca starch in a bowl.
2. Add the heavy cream and whole milk and whisk well to incorporate all of the dry ingredients into the liquid.
3. Add the corn syrup and apple pie filling. Blend with an immersion blender to incorporate the ingredients, making sure to blend the apple pie filling fully into the base.

Cook

4. Pour the mixture into a 2.5-quart / 2.36-liter saucepan, using a spatula to scrape the sides of the bowl. Place the saucepan on medium-high heat and cook, whisking continuously to prevent any burning or clumping. Whisk slowly in the beginning and increase speed as the mixture gets warmer and begins to steam and thicken. It should thicken without boiling after 8 to 12 minutes on the heat; watch carefully so it doesn't burn. Once the mixture has thickened enough to coat the back of a spoon, continue cooking 15 seconds longer, whisking vigorously. Then immediately remove from the heat.

Freeze

5. Pour the mixture into a clean glass or stainless-steel bowl and lay plastic wrap directly on the surface to prevent a skin from forming on top. Allow the mixture to sit 30 to 45 minutes, until no longer hot. Then place in the refrigerator to cool completely, about 4 hours. If the mixture needs to be used right away, submerge most of the bowl in an ice bath and let it sit 30 to 40 minutes, refreshing the ice as necessary.

6. Once the mixture has cooled completely and thickened further, pour it into the bowl of the gelato machine and churn the gelato according to the manufacturer's directions. The gelato will expand and should spin until it's thick and creamy but still soft enough to scoop into a storage container, about 30 to 55 minutes.

7. Use a rubber spatula to scoop the gelato into a storage container.

8. Press a piece of plastic wrap or parchment paper directly on the surface of the gelato, seal the container with an airtight lid, and put it in the freezer.

9. Freeze at least 4 to 5 hours. When ready, the gelato should be firm enough to scoop but soft and creamy in texture.

Serve

10. Enjoy the fresh gelato as soon as possible. If using after 1 day, allow 7 to 10 minutes for the gelato to soften outside of the freezer before eating.

Apple Pie Filling

Homemade vs. commercially made: cooked and caramelized apples in butter with sugar and cinnamon are what's needed for this gelato. If you like your own homemade filling, use it by all means. I find using a commercially produced apple pie filling speeds up the recipe, and most canned fillings have the right amount of spice and sweetness. There are many to choose from in supermarkets, but do use a brand you trust or have already tried.

AVOCADO
Avocado

Made on and in celebration of Cinco de Mayo at Morano Gelato, this nontraditional flavor is not so unusual in the ice cream world. Many have made avocado ice cream, and once you've tasted it, there's no surprise why. Avocado gelato is creamy, sweet, earthy—and bright green! Make sure to use a fresh and fully ripe avocado. The softer the avocado, the easier it will be to blend it into the gelato base.

Ingredients

2 ounces / 56 grams milk powder

7.05 ounces / 200 grams granulated sugar

1 pinch kosher salt

0.7 ounce / 20 grams tapioca starch

6.75 ounces / 192 grams heavy cream

24.15 ounces / 685 grams whole milk

1.15 ounces / 33 grams light corn syrup

4.7 ounces / 134 grams avocado, sliced (about 1 avocado)

Yield: About 1.5 quarts / 1.42 liters

Prepare

1. Mix the milk powder, sugar, salt, and tapioca starch in a bowl.
2. Add the heavy cream and whole milk and whisk well to incorporate all of the dry ingredients into the liquid.
3. Add the corn syrup and avocado. Blend with an immersion blender, making sure to fully incorporate all of the avocado pieces into the base. No large pieces should remain and most, if not all, of the avocado should be blended into the base.

Cook

4. Pour the mixture into a 2.5-quart / 2.36-liter saucepan, using a spatula to scrape the sides of the bowl. Place the saucepan on medium-high heat and cook, whisking continuously to prevent any burning or clumping. Whisk slowly in the beginning and increase speed as the mixture gets warmer and begins to steam and thicken. It should thicken without boiling after 8 to 12 minutes on the heat; watch carefully so it doesn't burn. Once the mixture has thickened enough to coat the back of a spoon, continue cooking 15 seconds longer, whisking vigorously. Then immediately remove from the heat.

Freeze

5. Pour the mixture into a clean glass or stainless-steel bowl and lay plastic wrap directly on the surface to prevent a skin from forming on top. Allow the mixture to sit 30 to 45 minutes, until no longer hot. Then place in the refrigerator to cool completely, about 4 hours. If the mixture needs to be used right away, submerge most of the bowl in an ice bath and let it sit 30 to 40 minutes, refreshing the ice as necessary.
6. Once the mixture has cooled completely and thickened further, pour it into the bowl of the gelato machine and churn the gelato according to the manufacturer's directions. The gelato will expand and should spin until it's thick and creamy but still soft enough to scoop into a storage container, about 30 to 55 minutes.
7. Use a rubber spatula to scoop the gelato into a storage container.
8. Press a piece of plastic wrap or parchment paper directly on the surface of the gelato, seal the container with an airtight lid, and put it in the freezer.
9. Freeze at least 4 to 5 hours. When ready, the gelato should be firm enough to scoop but soft and creamy in texture.

Serve

10. Enjoy the fresh gelato as soon as possible. If using after 1 day, allow 7 to 10 minutes for the gelato to soften outside of the freezer before eating.

BISCOFF
Belgian Spice Cookie

Biscoff cookies and spreads have developed a strong following in Europe and more recently in America, as more people travel and have the pleasure of tasting them. The spread should be available in specialty food stores next to the peanut butter and Nutella, but if you can't find it, you can order it (and the cookies) online (www.biscoff.com).

Ingredients

2 ounces / 56 grams milk powder

7.05 ounces / 200 grams granulated sugar

1 pinch kosher salt

0.7 ounce / 20 grams tapioca starch

6.75 ounces / 192 grams heavy cream

24.15 ounces / 685 grams whole milk

1.25 ounces / 36 grams light corn syrup

4.4 ounces / 125 grams Biscoff Spread (creamy style)

Biscoff cookies for garnish

Yield: About 1.5 quarts / 1.42 liters

Prepare

1. Mix the milk powder, sugar, salt, and tapioca starch in a bowl.

2. Add the heavy cream and whole milk and whisk well to incorporate all of the dry ingredients into the liquid.

3. Add the corn syrup and Biscoff Spread. Blend with an immersion blender so that the Biscoff Spread is fully incorporated into the base.

Cook

4. Pour the mixture into a 2.5-quart / 2.36-liter saucepan, using a spatula to scrape the sides of the bowl. Place the saucepan on medium-high heat and cook, whisking continuously to prevent any burning or clumping. Whisk slowly in the beginning and increase speed as the mixture gets warmer and begins to steam and thicken. It should thicken without boiling after 8 to10 minutes on the heat; watch carefully so it doesn't burn. Once the mixture has thickened enough to coat the back of a spoon, continue cooking 15 seconds longer, whisking vigorously. Then immediately remove from the heat.

Freeze

5. Pour the mixture into a clean glass or stainless-steel bowl and lay plastic wrap directly on the surface to prevent a skin from forming on top. Allow mixture to cool 30 to 45 minutes, until no longer hot. Then place in the refrigerator to cool completely, about 4 hours. If the mixture needs to be used right away, submerge most of the bowl in an ice bath and let it sit 30 to 40 minutes, refreshing the ice as necessary.

6. Once the mixture has cooled completely and thickened further, pour it into the bowl of the gelato machine and churn the gelato according to the manufacturer's directions. The gelato will expand and should spin until it's thick and creamy but still soft enough to scoop into a storage container, about 30 to 55 minutes.

7. Use a rubber spatula to scoop the gelato into a storage container.

8. Press a piece of plastic wrap or parchment paper directly on the surface of the gelato, seal the container with an airtight lid, and put it in the freezer.

9. Freeze at least 4 to 5 hours. When ready, the gelato should be firm enough to scoop but soft and creamy in texture.

Serve

10. Enjoy the fresh gelato as soon as possible. If using after 1 day, allow 7 to 10 minutes for the gelato to soften outside of the freezer before eating. If desired, crush or chop 3 to 4 (or more) Biscoff cookies and sprinkle on top of the gelato for garnish.

BURRO ROSOLATO
Brown Butter

One of my favorite nontraditional Italian flavors, Brown Butter gelato is made at Morano Gelato around Thanksgiving time. The sweetness of the milk base combined with the caramelized nuttiness of the butter creates an irresistible flavor that somehow seems perfect on cool days and firelit evenings.

A little extra prep time is needed to brown the butter (and a little practice, too, if you are not familiar with the technique of browning butter), but otherwise this recipe is simple, and the results are delicious.

Burro Rosolato gelato is perfect on any pie or fruit crisp, but I often eat it on its own with a little whipped cream. It's a great alternative to the usual sundae flavors as well.

Ingredients

3 ounces / 85 grams browned butter (about 1 stick)

2 ounces / 56 grams milk powder

6.35 ounces / 180 grams granulated sugar

2 pinches kosher salt

0.7 ounce / 20 grams tapioca starch

6.75 ounces / 192 grams heavy cream

24.15 ounces / 685 grams whole milk

1.15 ounces / 33 grams light corn syrup

Yield: About 1.5 quarts / 1.42 liters

Prepare

1. Slice a stick of butter into four equal pieces and place them in a skillet on medium heat. Shake the pan every other minute or so to ensure that each piece melts evenly. Keep shaking the pan occasionally once the butter begins to melt and foam, then turn the heat down to medium-low while the milk solids in the butter start to brown. Keep an eye on the butter. Once it has turned golden to dark brown and smells nutty, immediately remove the skillet from the heat and carefully pour the butter into a heatproof bowl. Allow the butter to cool for 15 minutes and then measure the amount needed into a separate bowl and set aside.

2. Mix the milk powder, sugar, salt, and tapioca starch in a bowl.

3. Add the heavy cream and whole milk and whisk well to incorporate all of the dry ingredients into the liquid.

4. Whisk in the corn syrup.

Cook

5. Pour the mixture into a 2.5-quart / 2.36-liter saucepan, using a spatula to scrape the sides of the bowl. Place the saucepan on medium-high heat and cook, whisking continuously to prevent any burning or clumping. Whisk slowly in the beginning and increase speed as the mixture gets warmer and begins to steam and thicken. It should thicken without boiling after 8 to 12 minutes on the heat; watch carefully so it doesn't burn. Once the mixture has thickened enough to coat the back of a spoon, continue cooking 15 seconds longer, whisking vigorously. Then immediately remove from the heat.

Freeze

6. Pour the mixture into a clean glass or stainless-steel bowl. Make sure the browned butter is still in liquid form. If not, microwave as needed (30 seconds to 1 minute) to melt. Whisk the butter into the hot base.

7. Lay plastic wrap directly on the surface to prevent a skin from forming on top. Allow the mixture to sit 30 to 45 minutes, until no longer hot. Then place in the refrigerator to cool completely, about 4 hours. If the mixture needs to be used right away, submerge most of the bowl in an ice bath and let it sit 30 to 40 minutes, refreshing the ice as necessary.

8. Once the mixture has cooled completely and thickened further, pour it into the bowl of the gelato machine and churn the gelato according to the manufacturer's directions. The gelato will expand and should spin until it's thick and creamy but still soft enough to scoop into a storage container, about 30 to 55 minutes.

9. Use a rubber spatula to scoop the gelato into a storage container.

10. Press a piece of plastic wrap or parchment paper directly on the surface of the gelato, seal the container with an airtight lid, and put it in the freezer.

11. Freeze at least 4 to 5 hours. When ready, the gelato should be firm enough to scoop but soft and creamy in texture.

Serve

12. Enjoy the fresh gelato as soon as possible. If using after 1 day, allow 8 to 12 minutes for the gelato to soften outside of the freezer before eating.

Browning Butter

Browning the butter requires a watchful eye because it can easily burn while melting, but I still suggest browning it as much as you comfortably can. The browner the butter, the deeper the flavor, but take care: any burned notes in the butter will carry over into the gelato.

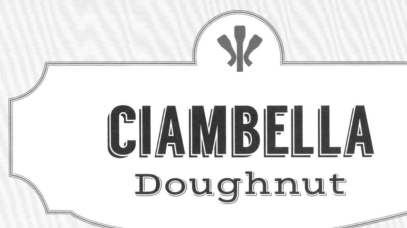

CIAMBELLA
Doughnut

At Morano Gelato, Ciambella is another flavor that only gets made once a year on the Fourth of July, just like Torta di Mele (page 140). I've always loved doughnuts, and I made this flavor with a particular doughnut in mind: a sugar-and-cinnamon-coated old-fashioned doughnut sold at a small store in Meriden, New Hampshire. These doughnuts are huge, and they have the perfect balance of sweetness and grease. They're also perfectly cooked, crunchy on the outside and cake-like on the inside.

The first day I made Ciambella, I strolled into the laboratory, doughnuts in hand, confident that it would work, and managed to get the recipe exactly how I wanted it on the first try. The employees and customers were impressed. Tasting Ciambella is just like biting into a doughnut—grease, sugar, and all—but without the crunch. Instead, a smooth and creamy finish helps remind you that this is, in fact, a much lighter treat than the doughnut itself.

Ciambella gelato will wow anyone who tries it—so much so that you may find yourself enjoying a scoop with a cup of coffee. Or you can pair it with our Italian Espresso gelato (page 40) for an all-in-one cup of breakfast that is sure to help start the day right.

Ingredients

2 ounces / 56 grams milk powder

6.7 ounces / 190 grams granulated sugar

1 pinch kosher salt

1 pinch ground nutmeg

1 pinch ground cinnamon

0.7 ounce / 20 grams tapioca starch

6.75 ounces / 192 grams heavy cream

24.15 ounces / 685 grams whole milk

1.15 ounces / 33 grams light corn syrup

4.10 ounces / 115 grams doughnut, broken into pieces

Whole donuts to serve with gelato

Yield: About 1.5 quarts / 1.42 liters

Prepare

1. Mix the milk powder, sugar, salt, nutmeg, cinnamon, and tapioca starch in a bowl.
2. Add the heavy cream and whole milk and whisk well to incorporate all of the dry ingredients into the liquid.
3. Add the corn syrup and doughnut pieces. Blend with an immersion blender, making sure to completely incorporate all the doughnut pieces into the base.

Cook

4. Pour the mixture into a 2.5-quart / 2.36-liter saucepan, using a spatula to scrape the sides of the bowl. Place the saucepan on medium-high heat and cook, whisking continuously to prevent any burning or clumping. Whisk slowly in the beginning and increase speed as the mixture gets warmer and begins to steam and thicken. It should thicken without boiling after 8 to 12 minutes on the heat; watch carefully so it doesn't burn. Once the mixture has thickened enough to coat the back of a spoon, continue cooking 15 seconds longer, whisking vigorously. Then immediately remove from the heat.

Freeze

5. Pour the mixture into a clean glass or stainless-steel bowl and lay plastic wrap directly on the surface to prevent a skin from forming on top. Allow the mixture to sit 30 to 45 minutes, until no longer hot. Then place in the refrigerator to cool completely, about 4 hours. If the mixture needs to be used right away, submerge most of the bowl in an ice bath and let it sit 30 to 40 minutes, refreshing the ice as necessary.

Doughnuts

Obviously for this flavor, the better the doughnut, the better the taste. Choose a cake-like donut that isn't too greasy. Sugar coating is fine but don't use doughnuts that are glazed or frosted.

6. Once the mixture has cooled completely and thickened further, pour it into the bowl of the gelato machine and churn the gelato according to the manufacturer's directions. The gelato will expand and should spin until it's thick and creamy but still soft enough to scoop into a storage container, about 30 to 55 minutes.

7. Use a rubber spatula to scoop the gelato into a storage container.

8. Press a piece of plastic wrap or parchment paper directly on the surface of the gelato, seal the container with an airtight lid, and put it in the freezer.

9. Freeze at least 4 to 5 hours. When ready, the gelato should be firm enough to scoop but soft and creamy in texture.

Serve

10. Enjoy the fresh gelato as soon as possible. If using after 1 day, allow 7 to 10 minutes for the gelato to soften outside of the freezer before eating.

ACERO
Maple

This nontraditional Italian flavor is made at Morano Gelato Hanover during the fall and spring in support of the local maple production. We use a dark grade-B syrup from Mac's Maple in Plainfield, New Hampshire. (Mac's also produces a bourbon maple syrup that is unbelievably good—and at Morano Gelato, we make this flavor, too.) When making Acero gelato, use the darkest syrup you can find for the best flavor results. Although I'm partial to maple syrup made in New Hampshire or Vermont, any quality syrup will work, no matter what the grade, as long as it is pure maple syrup.

I recommend making this flavor in the fall to complement a fresh-out-of-the-oven pie or a nice fruit crisp, or in the spring to celebrate the oncoming warm weather.

Ingredients

2 ounces / 56 grams milk powder

6 ounces / 170 grams granulated sugar

1 pinch kosher salt

0.7 ounce / 20 grams tapioca starch

7.4 ounces / 210 grams heavy cream

24.15 ounces / 685 grams whole milk

1 ounce / 28 grams light corn syrup

4.05 ounces / 115 grams maple syrup (grade B or darker recommended), plus extra for garnish (optional)

1 egg yolk

Yield: About 1.5 quarts / 1.42 liters

Prepare

1. Mix the milk powder, sugar, salt, and tapioca starch in a bowl

2. Add the heavy cream and whole milk and whisk well to incorporate all of the dry ingredients into the liquid.

3. Whisk in the corn syrup, maple syrup, and egg yolk.

Cook

4. Pour the mixture into a 2.5-quart / 2.36-liter saucepan, using a spatula to scrape the sides of the bowl. Place the saucepan on medium-high heat and cook, whisking continuously to prevent any burning or clumping. Whisk slowly in the beginning and increase speed as the mixture gets warmer and begins to steam and thicken. It should thicken without boiling after 8 to 12 minutes on the heat; watch carefully so it doesn't burn. Once the mixture has thickened enough to coat the back of a spoon, continue cooking 15 seconds longer, whisking vigorously. Then immediately remove from the heat.

Tip

Did you know that you can freeze maple syrup? Pure maple syrup does not freeze solid and can remain in the freezer indefinitely. Freezing prevents the formation of crystals and mold. Bring to room temperature before using.

Maple Syrup

Generally speaking, as the maple syrup season progresses, the color of the syrup gets darker. This is due to the changes in the maple tree as the weather gets warmer, and buds and leaves start to come out.

Freeze

5. Pour the mixture into a clean glass or stainless-steel bowl and lay plastic wrap directly on the surface to prevent a skin from forming on top. Allow the mixture to sit 30 to 45 minutes, until no longer hot. Then place in the refrigerator to cool completely, about 4 hours. If the mixture needs to be used right away, submerge most of the bowl in an ice bath and let it sit 30 to 40 minutes, refreshing the ice as necessary.

6. Once the mixture has cooled completely and thickened further, pour it into the bowl of the gelato machine and churn the gelato according to the manufacturer's directions. The gelato will expand and should spin until it's thick and creamy but still soft enough to scoop into a storage container, about 30 to 55 minutes.

7. Use a rubber spatula to scoop the gelato into a storage container.

8. Press a piece of plastic wrap or parchment paper directly on the surface of the gelato, seal the container with an airtight lid, and put it in the freezer.

9. Freeze at least 4 to 5 hours. When ready, the gelato should be firm enough to scoop but soft and creamy in texture.

Serve

10. Enjoy the fresh gelato as soon as possible. If using after 1 day, allow 5 to 8 minutes for the gelato to soften outside of the freezer before eating. Serve with additional maple syrup, if desired.

SORBETTO
Sorbet

LO SCIROPPO PER SORBETTO
Sorbet Syrup

Although there are many ways to make a sorbet, I prefer preparing a sorbet syrup to use as the base for each sorbet recipe. The syrup helps sweeten my sorbets while giving them a fuller body and creamier texture.

Even though sorbets are water based, and fruits contain even more water, discovering ways to make sorbets less icy has been a pursuit of mine for years at Morano Gelato. After much experimenting, I've developed recipes for fruit sorbets that customers often think are dairy based because of their creamy texture. This is due in part to the strong sorbet syrup.

You'll see that I've included tapioca starch in this recipe. Even though it's a small amount, it helps reduce crystallization. However, if you prefer to have no starch in the syrup, you can leave it out. This recipe makes enough syrup for a little over two batches of sorbet.

Ingredients

17.65 ounces / 500 grams granulated sugar

0.88 ounce / 25 grams tapioca starch

17.65 ounces / 500 grams water

4.05 ounces / 115 grams light corn syrup

Yield: About 1.16 quarts / 1 liter

Prepare

1. Mix the sugar and tapioca starch in a bowl.
2. Add the water and corn syrup and whisk well to incorporate the dry ingredients into the liquid.

Cook

3. Pour the mixture into a 2.5-quart / 2.36-liter saucepan, using a spatula to scrape the sides of the bowl. Place the saucepan on medium-high heat and cook, whisking continuously to prevent any burning or clumping. Whisk slowly in the beginning and increase speed as the mixture gets warmer and begins to steam. Cook the syrup for 12 to 15 minutes or until just before boiling. You should see a difference in the syrup once the sugar has dissolved. It should be thicker and more viscous. Once finished, remove immediately from the heat.

Cool

4. Pour the syrup into a clean glass or stainless-steel bowl. Allow it to sit 30 to 45 minutes, until no longer hot. Then cover the bowl with plastic wrap and place it in the refrigerator to cool completely before using, at least 4 hours.

Package

5. Transfer the syrup to a storage container with a tight-fitting lid and place it in the refrigerator until ready for use. The syrup can be kept in the refrigerator for up to 4 days. Whisk well prior to using.

BANANA
Banana

Due to the low water content and creaminess of the fruit, Banana is one of the smoothest sorbets we make at Morano Gelato. This sorbet is best with ripe (but not brown) bananas, or you can make it with green bananas if you're looking for a different and young-tasting banana flavor. You can add lemon juice to brighten the color and cut through the sweetness of the sorbet or enjoy it on the sweeter side, as is.

Banana sorbet is classically paired with Fior di Latte (page 30) or Cioccolato Fondente (page 48) gelato.

Ingredients

18.52 ounces / 525 grams banana, peeled and cut in half (about 6 bananas)

1.75 ounces / 50 grams cold water

17.64 ounces / 500 grams sorbet syrup (page 162), cooled and whisked prior to measuring

0.07 ounce / 2 grams fresh-squeezed lemon juice (optional)

Yield: About 1 quart / 950 milliliters

Prepare

1. Place the banana, water, sorbet syrup, and lemon juice, if using, in a bowl.
2. Blend well with an immersion blender, making sure to incorporate all the banana pieces into the liquid.

Freeze

3. Pour the mixture into the bowl of the gelato machine and churn the sorbet according to the manufacturer's directions. The sorbet will expand and should spin until thick but still soft enough to scoop into a storage container, about 30 to 55 minutes.
4. Using a rubber spatula, scoop the sorbet into a storage container.
5. Press a piece of plastic wrap or parchment paper directly on the surface of the sorbet, seal the container with an airtight lid, and put it in the freezer.
6. Freeze at least 4 to 5 hours. When ready, the sorbet should be firm enough to scoop but soft in texture.

Serve

7. Enjoy the fresh sorbet as soon as possible. If using the next day or after, allow at least 8 to 10 minutes for the sorbet to soften outside of the freezer before eating.

Tip

Try adding Banana sorbet to your favorite smoothie. It's a great way to thicken and add a flavor kick to any frozen blended fruit drink.

Bananas

Ethylene gas is what causes bananas to ripen. Want them to ripen faster? Put them in a brown bag where the gas will be concentrated or place them in a low-heat oven until brown spots appear on the skin (about an hour).

FRAGOLA
Strawberry

Fragola is a common sorbet flavor in Italy and is best made when strawberries are in season, fully ripe and juicy. I add a little lemon and orange juice to give the flavor more depth and to heighten the taste of the strawberries—at times, citrus does for fruit what salt does for savory dishes.

Ingredients

15.5 ounces / 440 grams strawberries, hulled and sliced into small pieces

1.75 ounces / 50 grams cold water

14.62 ounces / 415 grams sorbet syrup (page 162), cooled and whisked prior to measuring

0.1 ounce / 3 grams fresh-squeezed lemon juice

0.1 ounce / 3 grams fresh-squeezed orange juice

Yield: About 1 quart / 950 milliliters

Prepare

1. Place the strawberries, water, sorbet syrup, and lemon and orange juices in a bowl.
2. Blend well with an immersion blender to incorporate all the strawberry pieces into the liquid.

Freeze

3. Pour the mixture into the bowl of the gelato machine and churn the sorbet according to the manufacturer's directions. The sorbet will expand and should spin until thick but still soft enough to scoop into a storage container, about 30 to 55 minutes.
4. Using a rubber spatula, scoop the sorbet into a storage container.
5. Press a piece of plastic wrap or parchment paper directly on the surface of the sorbet, seal the container with an airtight lid, and put it in the freezer.
6. Freeze at least 4 to 5 hours. When ready, the sorbet should be firm enough to scoop but soft in texture.

Serve

7. Enjoy the fresh sorbet as soon as possible. If using the next day or after, allow at least 10 to 20 minutes for the sorbet to soften outside of the freezer before eating.

Strawberries

For a refreshing treat on a hot day, try blending Strawberry sorbet with sparkling water or with Prosecco for a light summer cocktail.

FRUTTI DI BOSCO
Forest Berries

Frutti di Bosco is the flavor that many who have visited Italian gelato shops seem to remember the most. Its dark red color with hints of blue and purple seems to intrigue viewers, and its bold berry flavor delights all who try it.

I use strawberries, blackberries, blueberries, and raspberries in this recipe, but any combination of berries will work.

Ingredients

2.8 ounces / 80 grams strawberries, hulled and sliced into small pieces

4.9 ounces / 140 grams raspberries, whole

3.9 ounces / 110 grams blueberries, whole

3.9 ounces / 110 grams blackberries, whole

2.1 ounces / 60 grams cold water

14.62 ounces / 415 grams sorbet syrup (page 162), cooled and whisked prior to measuring

0.1 ounce / 3 grams fresh-squeezed lemon juice

0.1 ounce / 3 grams fresh-squeezed orange juice

Yield: About 1 quart / 950 milliliters

Prepare

1. Place the berries, water, sorbet syrup, and lemon and orange juices in a bowl.
2. Blend well with an immersion blender, making sure to incorporate all the berry pieces into the liquid.

Freeze

3. Pour the mixture into the bowl of the gelato machine and churn the sorbet according to the manufacturer's directions. The sorbet will expand and should spin until thick but still soft enough to scoop into a storage container, about 30 to 55 minutes.
4. Using a rubber spatula, scoop the sorbet into a storage container.
5. Press a piece of plastic wrap or parchment paper directly on the surface of the sorbet, seal the container with an airtight lid, and put it in the freezer.
6. Freeze at least 4 to 5 hours. When ready, the sorbet should be firm enough to scoop but soft in texture.

Serve

7. Enjoy the fresh sorbet as soon as possible. If using the next day or after, allow at least 10 to 20 minutes for the sorbet to soften outside of the freezer before eating.

KIWI
Kiwi

The kiwi is one of my favorite fruits, and in a sorbet, it's almost irresistible to me. As one close friend has put it: "When eating this Kiwi sorbet, you can almost taste the fuzz of the skin of the fruit." Seriously. Try it! Kiwi will become your fruit sorbet of choice, and it's perfect on a hot summer day.

When it comes to choosing kiwis, size doesn't matter. Just look for fruits that are unblemished and give a little when you press the outside. Rock-hard kiwis are not ready to eat or to make into strong-flavored sorbet. Kiwis sweeten as they ripen, so make sure they've had plenty of time on your kitchen counter. The kiwi is a staple in my kitchen, so it's no wonder that I'm partial to its frozen form.

Kiwi sorbet is versatile, just like many of the other sorbets, and delicious all by itself. Try adding a scoop to your yogurt in the morning. It's also great midday snack and can help elevate a dessert course at a dinner party. Add a little dark chocolate gelato, and you'll have one of my favorite combinations.

Ingredients

16.9 ounces / 479 grams kiwi, peeled, ends removed, and diced (about 8 kiwis)

1.95 ounces / 55 grams cold water

13.95 ounces / 395 grams sorbet syrup (page 162), cooled and whisked prior to measuring

0.07 ounce / 2 grams fresh-squeezed lemon juice (optional)

Yield: About 1 quart / 950 milliliters

Prepare

1. Place the kiwi, water, sorbet syrup, and lemon juice, if using, in a small bowl.
2. Blend well with an immersion blender, making sure to incorporate all the kiwi pieces into the liquid..

Freeze

3. Pour the mixture into the bowl of the gelato machine and churn the sorbet according to the manufacturer's directions. The sorbet will expand and should spin until thick but still soft enough to scoop into a storage container, about 30 to 55 minutes.
4. Using a rubber spatula, scoop the sorbet into a storage container.
5. Press a piece of plastic wrap or parchment paper directly on the surface of the sorbet, seal the container with an airtight lid, and put it in the freezer.
6. Freeze at least 4 to 5 hours. When ready, the sorbet should be firm enough to scoop but soft in texture..

Serve

7. Enjoy the fresh sorbet as soon as possible. If using the next day or after, allow at least 10 to 20 minutes for the sorbet to soften outside of the freezer before eating.

Kiwi

As with other fruits, it's important to use the best possible kiwis and allow them to fully ripen to maximize their flavor potential prior to turning them into a sorbet. Make sure, however, that the kiwis still have some tang and firmness to them and aren't too soft or mushy. I encourage you to taste the fruit, and if you find it a little on the sweeter side, you can add a little lemon juice to help round out the flavor. Otherwise, if you prefer a sweet kiwi sorbet or believe the kiwis to be just right, follow the recipe as is. Enjoy!

Did You Know?

After China, Italy is the second largest producer of kiwi in the world. The Lazio region, home to Rome, exports the most of this fruit. It's no wonder Kiwi sorbet is everywhere in Italy!

LIMONE
Lemon

Limone is one of the most popular sorbet flavors we serve at Morano Gelato. Its tang is just sharp enough to make you pucker, but the sweet finish leaves you with the desire for more, especially on a warm day. For an additional kick, lime juice can be substituted for the lemon juice in this recipe. Just make sure the fruit you use is fresh. Lemon sorbet is as refreshing as it gets. Frozen lemonade soda (Lemon sorbet with a little sparkling water) got me through many long hours working at Morano Gelato Hanover during our hot and busy months.

Ingredients

16.2 ounces / 460 grams fresh-squeezed lemon juice, strained (about 11 lemons)

21.7 ounces / 615 grams sorbet syrup (page 162), cooled and whisked prior to measuring

Zest of 4 lemons, finely chopped

Yield: About 1 quart / 950 milliliters

Prepare

1. Place the lemon juice and sorbet syrup in a bowl.
2. Add the zest and whisk well.

Freeze

3. Pour the mixture into the bowl of the gelato machine and churn the sorbet according to the manufacturer's directions. The sorbet will expand and should spin until thick but still soft enough to scoop into a storage container, about 30 to 55 minutes.
4. Using a rubber spatula, scoop the sorbet into a storage container.
5. Press a piece of plastic wrap or parchment paper directly on the surface of the sorbet, seal the container with an airtight lid, and put it in the freezer.
6. Freeze at least 4 to 5 hours. When ready, the sorbet should be firm enough to scoop but soft in texture.

Serve

7. Enjoy the fresh sorbet as soon as possible. If using the next day or after, allow at least 10 to 20 minutes for the sorbet to soften outside of the freezer before eating.

Juicing Lemons

To get the maximum amount of juice out of lemons (or any citrus fruit for that matter), the fruit should be at room temperature, which makes it soft and easy to squeeze by hand. Before juicing, roll the fruit back and forth on the counter to break through some of the segments inside the fruit and make it easier to extract the juice.

MELONE
Cantaloupe

Melone is a quintessential Italian sorbet flavor that often, like Fior di Latte (page 30), tests the level of artistry at a gelato shop. It's not an easy flavor to make because of the water content in the fruit, so many shops often use an imitation cantaloupe flavor for the sorbet and add gigantic pieces of melon for garnish. Although it's difficult to achieve optimal results with a home gelato maker, I've created a simple recipe that showcases the cantaloupe without being too icy.

Ingredients

21 ounces / 595 grams cantaloupe, peeled, ends and seeds removed, and diced (about 1 melon)

1.75 ounces / 50 grams cold water

18.15 ounces / 515 grams sorbet syrup (page 162), cooled and whisked prior to measuring

Yield: About 1 quart / 950 milliliters

Prepare

1. Place the cantaloupe, water, and sorbet syrup in a bowl.
2. Blend well with an immersion blender, making sure to incorporate all the melon pieces into the liquid.

Freeze

3. Pour the mixture into the bowl of the gelato machine and churn the sorbet according to the manufacturer's directions. The sorbet will expand and should spin until thick but still soft enough to scoop into a storage container, about 30 to 55 minutes.
4. Using a rubber spatula, scoop the sorbet into a storage container.
5. Press a piece of plastic wrap or parchment paper directly on the surface of the sorbet, seal the container with an airtight lid, and put it in the freezer.
6. Freeze at least 4 to 5 hours. When ready, the sorbet should be firm enough to scoop but soft in texture.

Serve

7. Enjoy the fresh sorbet as soon as possible. If using the next day or after, allow at least 10 to 20 minutes for the sorbet to soften outside of the freezer before eating.

Cantaloupes

Shake and smell—that's the way to test a cantaloupe for ripeness. When you shake it, you should hear the seeds inside rattling. There should also be a pleasant cantaloupe aroma when you smell the stem end of the fruit.

PERA
Pear

At Morano Gelato, Pera is a flavor made in the fall and winter only, but in Italy, it is often served throughout the year. I use Bosc pears, both because they ripen well and give a strong pear flavor, however, any type of fully ripe pear will work, as long as it has a bold flavor. After all, this sorbet recipe, like the other sorbet recipes is all about the fruit.

Ingredients

16.17 ounces / 459 grams pear, peeled, cored, ends removed, and diced (about 5 pears)

3.08 ounces / 88 grams cold water

14.8 ounces / 420 grams sorbet syrup (page 162), cooled and whisked prior to measuring

0.18 ounce / 5 grams fresh-squeezed lemon juice

Yield: About 1 quart / 950 milliliters

Prepare

1. Place the pear, water, sorbet syrup, and lemon juice in a bowl.
2. Blend well with an immersion blender, making sure to incorporate all the pear pieces into the liquid.

Freeze

3. Pour the mixture into the bowl of the gelato machine and churn the sorbet according to the manufacturer's directions. The sorbet will expand and should spin until thick but still soft enough to scoop into a storage container, about 30 to 55 minutes.
4. Using a rubber spatula, scoop the sorbet into a storage container.
5. Press a piece of plastic wrap or parchment paper directly on the surface of the sorbet, seal the container with an airtight lid, and put it in the freezer.
6. Freeze at least 4 to 5 hours. When ready, the sorbet should be firm enough to scoop but soft in texture.

Serve

7. Enjoy the fresh sorbet as soon as possible. If using the next day or after, allow at least 10 to 20 minutes for the sorbet to soften outside of the freezer before eating.

Pears

Use the ripest pears for peak flavor. Pears give off ethylene gas. To speed the ripening process, place them in a brown paper bag (which concentrates the gas) along with a banana, an avocado, or other fruit that also gives off ethylene gas.

ARANCIA
Orange

Any oranges will work for this sorbet recipe, even blood oranges, but it's important that the juice be freshly squeezed (by hand or with a juicing machine) and strained to prevent any unwanted seeds from being mixed into the sorbet. When in season, mandarin oranges can be made into a delicious Arancia sorbet. I recommend peeling, blending (with an immersion blender or regular blender), and then straining the mandarin orange juice for the best results.

Ingredients

16.2 ounces / 460 grams fresh-squeezed orange
   juice, strained (about 8 oranges)

22.6 ounces / 640 grams sorbet syrup
   (page 162), cooled and whisked prior
   to measuring

Zest of 1-1/2 oranges, finely chopped

Yield: About 1 quart / 950 milliliters

Prepare

1. Place the orange juice and sorbet syrup in a bowl.
2. Add the zest and whisk well.

Freeze

3. Pour the mixture into the bowl of the gelato machine and churn the sorbet according to the manufacturer's directions. The sorbet will expand and should spin until thick but still soft enough to scoop into a storage container, about 30 to 55 minutes.
4. Using a rubber spatula, scoop the sorbet into a storage container.
5. Press a piece of plastic wrap or parchment paper directly on the surface of the sorbet, seal the container with an airtight lid, and put it in the freezer.
6. Freeze at least 4 to 5 hours. When ready, the sorbet should be firm enough to scoop but soft in texture.

Serve

7. Enjoy the fresh sorbet as soon as possible. If using the next day or after, allow at least 10 to 20 minutes for the sorbet to soften outside of the freezer before eating.

Blood Oranges

Blood oranges originated in Sicily. They get their red color from a pigment called anthocyanin, which is a powerful antioxidant. The same pigment can be found in cherries and red cabbage.

PROSECCO
Italian Champagne

P rosecco is a fun sorbet flavor to make when entertaining guests or planning a romantic dinner. Any prosecco will work for this sorbet, as will French Champagne. This recipe does contain alcohol, with the content slightly over 25 percent, so be forewarned!

Since alcohol lowers the freezing point of the sorbet, I've added enough water to compensate and allow the sorbet to freeze without compromising the flavor of the prosecco. For a citrus-flavor twist, you can add the zest of one lemon or orange before freezing, if desired.

Ingredients

10.05 ounces / 285 grams prosecco

10.75 ounces / 305 grams cold water

11.10 ounces / 315 grams sorbet syrup (page 162), cooled and whisked prior to measuring

Yield: About 1 quart / 950 milliliters

Prepare

1. Whisk together the prosecco, water, and sorbet syrup in a bowl.

Freeze

2. Pour the mixture into the bowl of the gelato machine and churn the sorbet according to the manufacturer's directions. The sorbet will expand and should spin until thick but still soft enough to scoop into a storage container, about 30 to 55 minutes.

3. Using a rubber spatula, scoop the sorbet into a storage container.

4. Press a piece of plastic wrap or parchment paper directly on the surface of the sorbet, seal the container with an airtight lid, and put it in the freezer.

5. Freeze at least 4 to 5 hours. When ready, the sorbet should be firm enough to scoop but soft in texture.

Serve

6. Enjoy the fresh sorbet as soon as possible. If using the next day or after, allow at least 10 to 15 minutes for the sorbet to soften outside of the freezer before eating.

LAMPONE
Raspberry

Lampone has quickly become one of my favorite sorbet flavors—I love the flecks of seeds in each bite. And each summer at Morano Gelato, I was spoiled with deliveries of freshly picked raspberries from a local farm. Their perfume alone made the sorbet amazing, but the sorbet syrup gave the raspberries the sweetness they needed to send the flavor soaring to new heights. Any raspberries will work with this recipe, even golden or black. Just make sure the raspberries are in season and full of flavor to achieve the best results possible.

Ingredients

15.5 ounces / 440 grams raspberries, whole
(about 2.5 pints / 1.2 liters)

1.75 ounces / 50 grams cold water

14.62 ounces / 415 grams sorbet syrup
(page 162), cooled and whisked prior
to measuring

Yield: About 1 quart / 950 milliliters

Prepare

1. Place the raspberries, water, and sorbet syrup in a bowl.
2. Blend well with an immersion blender, making sure to incorporate all the raspberry pieces into the liquid.

Freeze

3. Pour the mixture into the bowl of the gelato machine and churn the sorbet according to the manufacturer's directions. The sorbet will expand and should spin until thick but still soft enough to scoop into a storage container, about 30 to 55 minutes.
4. Using a rubber spatula, scoop the sorbet into a storage container.
5. Press a piece of plastic wrap or parchment paper directly on the surface of the sorbet, seal the container with an airtight lid, and put it in the freezer.
6. Freeze at least 4 to 5 hours. When ready, the sorbet should be firm enough to scoop but soft in texture.

Serve

7. Enjoy the fresh sorbet as soon as possible. If using the next day or after, allow at least 10 to 20 minutes for the sorbet to soften outside of the freezer before eating.

Raspberries

Raspberries contain powerful antioxidants that are thought not only to help prevent cancer but, according to recent research, may even encourage cancerous cells to die and precancerous ones to remain noncancerous.

NUOVI GUSTI
New Flavors

LAVANDA
Lavender

Lavender is one of my favorite floral flavors. We added this gelato to the flavor list at Morano Gelato Hanover after numerous requests, and we started with a lavender extract from France that was gifted to me by a friend. After we had used the entire bottle, we had difficulty finding a replacement, until our kitchen manager in Hanover discovered a fragrant and delicate extract at Beanilla, an online purveyor of vanilla beans and quality extracts. We tested it, and it was perfect!

Although any lavender extract will work, make sure you pour it slowly. If using a brand other than the one we recommend, taste the gelato mixture every 5 grams when measuring to make sure the flavor is to your liking. This recipe, like all of the recipes in this book, is adjustable. I prefer our Lavender gelato to be similar to our Jasmine flavor, in that its creamy texture is not overpowered by the floral notes. Elegant enough to be served at a dinner party on a warm summer night, this gelato is not so intense in flavor as to turn off those who do not like the taste of lavender. If you like a stronger flavor, add more lavender.

Lavender is a wonderful flavor on its own, combined with berries and mint, or paired with a glass of prosecco. This gelato also makes a beautiful presentation when garnished with fresh or dried lavender flowers.

Lavender

A member of the mint family, lavender has been prized since ancient times for its healing and antiseptic qualities, and has been used to aid digestion, soothe headaches, and calm nerves. Today, this Old World native is valued for its sweet fragrance and delicate flavor with notes of citrus. The potency of lavender flowers increases when the buds are dried, so take a light hand when garnishing with dried lavender.

Ingredients

2.30 ounces / 65 grams milk powder

6.35 ounces / 180 grams granulated sugar

1.25 ounces / 35 grams tapioca starch

6.70 ounces / 190 grams heavy cream

24.15 ounces / 685 grams whole milk

0.90 ounces / 25 grams light corn syrup

0.42 ounces / 12 grams lavender extract

Yield: About 1.5 quarts / 1.42 liters

Prepare

1. Mix the milk powder, sugar, and tapioca starch in a bowl.
2. Add the heavy cream and whole milk and whisk well to incorporate all of the dry ingredients into the liquid.
3. Whisk in the corn syrup and lavender extract.

Cook

4. Pour the mixture into a 2.5-quart / 2.36-liter saucepan, using a spatula to scrape the sides of the bowl. Place the saucepan on medium-high heat and cook, whisking continuously to prevent any burning or clumping. Whisk slowly in the beginning and increase speed as the mixture gets warmer and begins to steam and thicken. The mixture should visibly thicken without boiling after 8 to 12 minutes on the heat. Once the mixture has thickened enough to coat the back of a spoon, continue cooking 15 seconds longer, whisking vigorously. Then remove from the heat immediately to prevent burning.

Freeze

5. Pour the mixture into a clean glass or stainless-steel bowl and lay plastic wrap directly on the surface to prevent a skin from forming on top. Allow the mixture to cool 30 to 45 minutes, until no longer hot. Then place in the refrigerator to cool completely, about 4 hours. If the mixture needs to be used right away, submerge most of the bowl into an ice bath and let the mixture sit 30 to 40 minutes, refreshing the ice as necessary.

6. Once the mixture has cooled completely and thickened further, pour it into the bowl of the gelato machine and churn the gelato according to the manufacturer's directions. The gelato will expand and should spin until it is thick and creamy but still soft enough to scoop into a storage container, about 30 to 55 minutes.

7. Using a rubber spatula, scoop the gelato into a storage container.

8. Press a piece of plastic wrap or parchment paper directly on the surface of the gelato, seal the container with an airtight lid, and place it in the freezer.

9. Freeze until firm, at least 4 to 5 hours. When ready, the gelato should be firm enough to scoop but soft and creamy in texture.

Serve

10. Enjoy the fresh gelato as soon as possible. If using after 1 day, allow the gelato to soften outside of the freezer for 8 to 10 minutes before eating.

CAFFÈ E MIELE
Italian Espresso and Honey

This recipe is a wonderful twist on a classic Italian flavor. Adding honey to espresso or coffee is not unusual, but the combination is rare in the frozen-dessert world. The key to this recipe is using the highest-quality espresso and honey you can find, and brewing, the espresso fresh. At Morano Gelato, we prefer Illy espresso and Ciboreale multiflower honey. (Ciboreale is new to the American market and thus may be difficult to find, but it's some of the best honey I've tasted.)

To elevate the flavor even more, garnish the gelato with fresh honeycomb and pair it with Fior di Latte gelato (page 30) to cut the sweetness, or add unsweetened panna (whipped cream).

Ingredients

2.30 ounces / 65 grams milk powder

3.50 ounces / 100 grams granulated sugar

0.15 ounces / 4 grams espresso grounds

1.25 ounces / 35 grams tapioca starch

7.60 ounces / 215 grams heavy cream

21.15 ounces / 600 grams whole milk

0.90 ounces / 25 grams light corn syrup

3.0 ounces / 85 grams brewed and
    cooled espresso (just over 1 shot)

3.17 ounces / 90 grams honey

1 egg yolk

Yield: About 1.5 quarts / 1.42 liters

Prepare

1. Mix the milk powder, sugar, espresso grounds, and tapioca starch in a bowl.
2. Add the heavy cream and whole milk to the bowl and whisk well to incorporate all of the dry ingredients into the liquid.
3. Whisk in the corn syrup, espresso, honey, and egg yolk.

Cook

4. Pour the mixture into a 2.5-quart / 2.36-liter saucepan, using a spatula to scrape the sides of the bowl. Place the saucepan on medium-high heat and cook, whisking continuously to prevent any burning or clumping. Whisk slowly in the beginning and increase speed as the mixture gets warmer and begins to steam and thicken. It should visibly thicken without boiling after 8 to 12 minutes on the heat. Once the mixture has thickened enough to coat the back of a spoon, continue cooking 15 seconds longer, whisking vigorously. Then remove from the heat immediately.

Freeze

5. Pour the mixture into a clean glass or stainless-steel bowl and lay plastic wrap directly on the surface to prevent a skin from forming on top. Allow the mixture to cool 30 to 45 minutes, until no longer hot. Then place it in the refrigerator to cool completely, about 4 hours. If the mixture needs to be used right away, submerge most of the bowl into an ice bath and let it sit 30 to 40 minutes, refreshing the ice as necessary.
6. Once the mixture has cooled completely and thickened further, pour it into the bowl of the gelato machine and churn the gelato according to the manufacturer's directions. The gelato will expand and should spin until it is thick and creamy but still soft enough to scoop into a storage container, about 30 to 55 minutes.
7. Using a rubber spatula, scoop the gelato into a storage container.
8. Press a piece of plastic wrap or parchment paper directly on the surface of the gelato, seal the container with an airtight lid, and put it in the freezer.
9. Freeze until firm, at least 4 to 5 hours. When ready, the gelato should be firm enough to scoop but soft and creamy in texture.

Serve

10. Enjoy the fresh gelato as soon as possible. If using after 1 day, allow the gelato to soften outside of the freezer for 8 to 10 minutes before eating.

MERINGA
Meringue

A bit sweeter than our Fior di Latte gelato (page 30), this recipe combines the creaminess of gelato with the crunchy texture of meringue pieces. With its subtle hint of vanilla, Meringa gelato is the perfect choice to serve with fresh peaches or cherries in season. I prefer pairing Italian Amarena cherries with this gelato—the sour cherries help balance the sweetness of this flavor, making it the perfect midday snack.

For those looking for a classic "American vanilla" recipe, this is very close!

Ingredients

2.30 ounces / 65 grams milk powder

5.64 ounces / 160 grams granulated sugar

1.25 ounces / 35 grams tapioca starch

2.65 ounces / 75 grams small meringue cookies (store bought or homemade), finely chopped

6.70 ounces / 190 grams heavy cream

24.15 ounces / 685 grams whole milk

0.90 ounce / 25 grams light corn syrup

0.18 ounces / 5 grams vanilla extract

Yield: About 1.5 quarts / 1.42 liters

Prepare

1. Mix the milk powder, sugar, tapioca starch, and meringue pieces in a bowl.
2. Add the heavy cream and whole milk and whisk well, incorporating all of the dry ingredients into the liquid.
3. Whisk in the corn syrup and vanilla extract.

Cook

4. Pour the mixture into a 2.5-quart / 2.36-liter saucepan, using a spatula to scrape the sides of the bowl. Place the saucepan on medium-high heat and cook, whisking continuously to prevent any burning or clumping. Whisk slowly in the beginning and increase speed as the mixture gets warmer and begins to steam and thicken. It should thicken without boiling after 8 to 12 minutes on the heat. Once the mixture has thickened enough to coat the back of a spoon, continue cooking 15 seconds longer, whisking vigorously. Then remove from the heat immediately.

Freeze

5. Pour the mixture into a clean glass or stainless-steel bowl and lay plastic wrap directly on the surface to prevent a skin from forming on top. Allow the mixture to cool 30 to 45 minutes, until no longer hot. Then place in the refrigerator to cool completely, about 4 hours. If the mixture needs to be used right away, submerge most of the bowl into an ice bath and let it sit 30 to 40 minutes, refreshing the ice as necessary.
6. Once the mixture has cooled completely and thickened further, pour it into the bowl of the gelato machine and churn the gelato according to the manufacturer's directions. The gelato will expand and should spin until it is thick and creamy but still soft enough to scoop into a storage container, about 30 to 55 minutes.
7. Using a rubber spatula, scoop the gelato into a storage container.
8. Press a piece of plastic wrap or parchment paper directly on the surface of the gelato, seal the container with an airtight lid, and place it in the freezer.
9. Freeze until firm, at least 4 to 5 hours. When ready, the gelato should be firm enough to scoop but soft and creamy in texture.

Serve

10. Enjoy the fresh gelato as soon as possible. If using after 1 day, allow the gelato to soften outside of the freezer for 8 to 10 minutes before eating.

CIOCCOLATO AL LATTE
Milk Chocolate

When I first began developing recipes for Morano Gelato, I created a darker chocolate that I loved, but that was a little intense for some of my customers. Within a few months, I had a lot of regulars asking for a milk-chocolate gelato, and I developed a recipe similar to the one below.

Cioccolato al Latte has become incredibly popular in our shops, and is the perfect chocolate flavor for layering in recipes such as Baked Alaska (page 199). It's a wonderful choice for chocolate lovers looking for a lighter yet deeply satisfying flavor.

Ingredients

1.25 ounces / 35 grams milk powder

7.95 ounces / 225 grams granulated sugar

0.05 ounce / 2 grams kosher salt
   (2 small pinches)

0.88 ounce / 25 grams tapioca starch

0.71 ounce / 20 grams cacao powder

6.70 ounces / 190 grams heavy cream

24.15 ounces / 685 grams whole milk

0.90 ounce / 25 grams light corn syrup

1.40 ounces / 40 grams 60% chocolate, finely
   chopped

1 egg yolk

Yield: About 1.5 quarts / 1.42 liters

Prepare

1. Mix the milk powder, sugar, salt, tapioca starch, and cacao powder in a bowl.
2. Add the heavy cream and whole milk and whisk well, incorporating all of the dry ingredients into the liquid.
3. Whisk in the corn syrup, chocolate, and egg yolk.

Cook

4. Pour the mixture into a 2.5-quart / 2.36-liter saucepan, using a spatula to scrape the sides of the bowl. Place the saucepan on medium-high heat and cook, whisking continuously to prevent any burning or clumping. Whisk slowly in the beginning and increase speed as the mixture gets warmer and begins to steam and thicken. It should thicken without boiling after 8 to 12 minutes on the heat. Once the mixture has thickened enough to coat the back of a spoon, continue cooking 15 seconds longer, whisking vigorously. Then remove from the heat immediately.

Freeze

5. Pour the mixture into a clean glass or stainless-steel bowl and lay plastic wrap directly on the surface to prevent a skin from forming on top. Allow the mixture to cool 30 to 45 minutes, until no longer hot. Then place the mixture in the refrigerator to cool completely, about 4 hours. If the mixture needs to be used right away, submerge most of the bowl into an ice bath and let it sit 30 to 40 minutes, refreshing the ice as necessary.
6. Once the mixture has cooled completely and thickened further, pour it into the bowl of the gelato machine and churn the gelato according to the manufacturer's directions. The gelato will expand and should spin until it is thick and creamy but still soft enough to scoop into a storage container, about 30 to 55 minutes.
7. Using a rubber spatula, scoop the gelato into a storage container.
8. Press a piece of plastic wrap or parchment paper directly on the surface of the gelato, seal the container with an airtight lid, and place it in the freezer.
9. Freeze until firm, at least 4 to 5 hours. When ready, the gelato should be firm enough to scoop but soft and creamy in texture.

Serve

10. Enjoy the fresh gelato as soon as possible. If using after 1 day, allow the gelato to soften outside of the freezer for 8 to 10 minutes before eating.

BAKED ALASKA

Milk Chocolate Gelato, Strawberry Sorbet, and Toasted Meringue

Baked Alaska is a new flavor we introduced at Morano Gelato in 2017. It combines layers of Milk-Chocolate gelato (page 196), tangy and sweet Strawberry sorbet (page 166), gooey Italian meringue, and sponge cake to create a unique dessert that stands out from our simple but bold gelato flavors.

You can prepare this recipe for a dinner party in any dish you prefer. We recommend a trifle dish to really wow your guests, but to start, try using an 8-inch / 20-cm round glass baking dish. Toasting the meringue with a kitchen torch highlights designs or patterns in the topping and creates a pleasing crisp layer.

Ingredients

½ batch Cioccolato al Latte (Milk-Chocolate) gelato recipe (page 196)

¾ batch Fragola (Strawberry) sorbet recipe (page 166)

2–4 cups / 475–950 milliliters Italian meringue (page 201)

2 cups / 120 grams crumbled high-quality sponge cake or yellow cake (store bought or freshly baked)

Yield: 1 8-inch / 20-cm round layered gelato

Assemble

1. Prepare the Cioccolato al Latte gelato recipe through step 6. Straight from the gelato machine, layer the mixture into the bottom half of a 8-inch / 20-cm round glass baking dish.

2. Press a piece of plastic wrap or parchment paper directly on the surface of the mixture, and place in the freezer. Freeze for 2 hours.

3. While the Cioccolato al Latte gelato is freezing, prepare the Fragola sorbet recipe through step 3.

4. Remove the Cioccolato al Latte gelato from the freezer after 2 hours. Sprinkle about half of the crumbled sponge cake over the surface of the Cioccolato al Latte gelato.

5. Once the Fragola sorbet is finished churning, layer it over the frozen Cioccolato al Latte gelato and sponge cake so that it almost reaches to the top of the dish.

6. Sprinkle the remaining pieces of sponge cake over the surface of the Fragola sorbet.

7. Freeze, covered with plastic wrap, for another 3 hours, until semi-firm and easy to scoop.

8. Shortly before the gelato is ready to be removed from the freezer, prepare the Italian meringue.

9. Once the meringue is ready, remove the gelato from the freezer and spread the meringue generously over the surface of the gelato using a spatula. Although 2 to 3 cups / 475 to 713 ml should be enough to cover the surface of an 8-inch / 20-cm dish, add meringue as needed to cover the entire surface of the gelato; form peaks by swirling and lifting the spatula over the meringue.

10. Using a butane kitchen torch, lightly toast the entire surface of the Italian meringue, being careful not to burn the peaks. It's important to work quickly, holding the torch about 2 inches / 5 centimeters from the meringue. You want to give the meringue peaks a nice golden color without melting the gelato.

Serve

11. Serve the fresh gelato immediately, scooping through all 5 layers (top to bottom) for each serving.

ITALIAN MERINGUE

This basic Italian meringue recipe works well with our Baked Alaska gelato. Double the recipe if you prefer extra meringue with your gelato.

Ingredients

½ cup / 100 grams granulated sugar

¼ cup water / 60 milliliters

2½ egg whites, at room temperature

¼ teaspoon cream of tartar

1½ teaspoons vanilla extract or seeds scraped from ½ vanilla bean pod

Yield: About 2 cups / 475 milliters

1. Over medium-high heat, combine the sugar and water in a small saucepan, stir once, and boil until the syrup reads 235°F / 112°C on a candy thermometer. Make sure to brush down the sides of the saucepan with a pastry brush dipped in water to prevent the syrup from crystallizing.

2. While the syrup is heating, combine the egg whites and cream of tartar in a mixer fitted with a whisk attachment. Whisk on low speed for 1 minute to mix the two ingredients, then increase speed to medium-high and beat until soft peaks form, about 2 to 4 minutes.

3. Remove syrup from the heat, set the mixer to medium-low speed, and slowly and carefully drizzle in the hot syrup.

4. Once all of the syrup has been incorporated, add the vanilla and switch the speed to medium-high

Index

Acknowledgments

The opportunity to write this book came as a surprise to me, and I jumped at it, knowing how often Morano Gelato customers look for recipes to make at home. So, first and foremost, I'm thankful to Nancy Hall and Race Point Publishing for having faith in Morano Gelato and my ability to write a book, along with everyone who helped put it together. To Chad Finer, the photographer—thank you so much for being willing to participate in such a large project and for making the gelato look beautiful. I'd also like to thank Mapleview Farm in Sutton, Massachusetts, for the barn board used for the cover shot. To my mother, who served as my transcriber when I foolishly dislocated my right shoulder as the book deadline approached—thank you for always being there when I need you. The same goes for my siblings, my huge extended family on both sides, and my friends. To all of the old and new employees of Morano Gelato Hanover who enthusiastically support Morano Gelato and what it stands for, and equally important, the customers who have watched and helped Morano Gelato grow over the years—thank you so much for your support and for helping Morano Gelato become what it is today. Last, to my best friend (you know who you are)—thank you for your unconditional support, encouragement, and help in eating all of my gelato experiments.

This book is dedicated in loving memory of my father and grandparents, Cosimo and Carmela Morano, who taught me the value of a strong work ethic and the importance of following one's dreams.